ULTIMATE WINNING SEASON

ULTIMATE WINNING SEASON

Transform Your Athlete's Talent into Leadership, Legacy, and NIL Success

NEELEY NEAL

ULTIMATE WINNING SEASON
Transform Your Athlete's Talent into Leadership, Legacy, and NIL Success

Copyright © 2025 by Neeley Neal

All rights reserved. No part of this book may be reproduced, distributed, or transmitted in any form or by any means, including photocopying, recording, or other electronic or mechanical methods, without the written permission from the publisher or author, except as permitted by U.S. copyright law or in the case of brief quotations embodied in a book review.

Disclaimer: Although the publisher and the author have made every effort to ensure that the information in this book was correct at press time and while this publication is designed to provide accurate information in regard to the subject matter covered, the publisher and the author assume no responsibility for errors, inaccuracies, omissions, or any other inconsistencies herein and hereby disclaim any liability to any party for any loss, damage, or disruption caused by errors or omissions, whether such errors or omissions result from negligence, accident, or any other cause.

Cover Design by Michael Nagin
Interior Layout and Design by Stephanie Anderson
Developmental and Copy Editing by Jeff Miller
Proofreading by Kiska Carr

ISBNs:
979-8-89165-235-4 *Paperback*
979-8-89165-236-1 *Hardback*
979-8-89165-237-8 *E-book*

Published by:
Streamline Books
Kansas City, MO
streamlinebookspublishing.com

*To Mom and Dad,
who taught me that true success is about
character, not just achievement.*

*To my husband, Dan,
my greatest teammate and strongest supporter.*

*And to Alex, Arthur, Bennett, and Henry—
may you always play the long game of life
with passion, purpose, and integrity.*

CONTENTS

Introduction ix

PART ONE: THE CHANGING LANDSCAPE

1   VUCA (Volatile, Uncertain, Complex, and Ambiguous) 3
2   Agility for the Win 11
3   Resilience + Growth 21
4   Transitions 29

PART TWO: BUILDING A PLATFORM FOR ULTIMATE SUCCESS

5   The Power of a Platform 43
6   The Real NIL Opportunity 53
7   Platformula for Success 67
8   Short-Term Gains Versus Long-Term Success 85
9   Don't Leave Potential on the Table 93
10 Values and Alignment 103
11 Relationships 115
12 What Does Success Look Like? 127

Conclusion 137
Ultimate Winning Season—Reader's Guide 141
About the Author 169
Endnotes 173

INTRODUCTION

CHANGE IS HAPPENING at an accelerated rate in every area of life, and since it shows no sign of slowing down, we must get ready to tackle it head-on and make the most of it.

Let's approach change without fear and embrace the opportunities it brings so we can set ourselves and our children up for success no matter what comes our way. After all, challenges and unexpected twists and turns aren't a matter of "if" but "when."

I wrote this book primarily for the parents of elite student athletes because our young athletes are stepping into an unprecedented time of challenge and opportunity in their lives. The world of college sports, as well as the world at large, is experiencing change at breakneck speed. Many parents feel like they're navigating a sea of uncertainty, ill-equipped and overwhelmed by all of the immense decisions that must be made and the life-changing growth their children are about to face.

As a parent, you are your child's first mentor and biggest fan. You were probably the first to spot their exceptional talent and potential, and you've been cheering them on ever since with optimism. However, optimism can be overshadowed by self-doubt and fear about your own adequacy. As the waves of change crash over you and your child, do you worry about your ability to handle it—or their ability to navigate the future?

Many parents fear they're not doing enough to nurture their child's potential. And let's face it: There aren't a lot of resources out there for parents of young athletes during this critical period in their lives. Who's mentoring the mentors? To put it another way, you are the Yoda to your young Luke Skywalker, but who is Yoda's Yoda?

Parents also worry about who will lead their children once they leave home. What kind of playbook will their new mentors—teachers, coaches, sports heroes—follow? And what if their game plan doesn't align with your family values? What if these new influences lead your child down an undesirable path?

Additionally, parents worry about their children losing their drive or getting distracted by the hustle and bustle of college life without the constant push to reach their potential. Just as one wrong move on the field can cost a team the game, a single, bad life decision during college could derail your child's trajectory, and we all know college students are prone to make some impulsive decisions.

How can we ensure our children are capable of making good decisions, using discernment, and putting their time and talents to good use when there's no predictable playbook for the future anymore? As parents, we know our children have a limited window of time to set themselves up for long-term success, so we feel a sense of urgency to encourage them to be action oriented and make the most of this time.

So what can we do? As parents, we must find ways to mitigate the risks while keeping an open, supportive relationship with our kids. They need to feel comfortable discussing their concerns and decisions with us. Even if they don't always

INTRODUCTION

show it, and even as our role evolves, our kids still need us as they transition into college life.

The constant social pressures, amplified by the online world and always-on nature of technology, often contribute to anxiety, mental health battles, and poor decisions. Parents, too, feel the strain of being constantly available and trying to keep up with the rapid pace of communication. It's a lot to handle.

But that's exactly why I wrote this book. I want to be a resource for you and for your family's success. I want to "mentor the mentors" (a Yoda for the Yodas) by providing you with clarity, actionable strategies, and a toolkit so you can become the supportive, guiding figure your children need as they transition from childhood to adulthood on a fast-moving stage.

Believe it or not, we are incredibly fortunate to be living in this time. The unknowns may be daunting, but I'm going to show you how to confidently navigate the challenges so you and your children can make the most of this amazing time in their lives. Let's get out there and win together.

And my advice isn't just for parents. Coaches, teachers, and anyone who mentors young people can also benefit from the strategies in this book. I'll show you how to help young athletes by creating dynamic, developmental environments where our future leaders can push their limits and grow in a supported but accelerated and strategic way.

Maximizing their potential means building a solid platform where they can leverage their unique gifts and talents at increasing scale throughout their lives and beyond sports. Later on, I'll guide you through creating a step-by-step roadmap for doing this with confidence and clarity.

Remember: This isn't a solo mission but a team effort. Relationships are essential to growth and making a real impact. So we'll also dive into how you and your child can shift from a competitive to a collaborative mindset. In a collaborative landscape, everyone rises together, supporting and lifting each other up. That's where the magic happens, where true growth and lasting impact come to life.

MY OWN EXPERIENCE

This subject is near and dear to my heart because I've seen the struggle, the challenges, and the opportunities from many different angles. I went from cheering on the NFL sidelines as a captain at Super Bowl XLIII to running multichannel marketing campaigns for one of the biggest brands in the "Big Game." Reflecting on my own experiences, I see how crucial my mentors were. Yet, the skills to succeed took me over a decade to master. If I'd had the guidance and resources I'm sharing with you now, I would have gotten there much faster and maximized the opportunities those doors opened for me.

I'm grateful for the perspective and experiences that brought me here. And now I want to open your eyes to the enormous opportunities this VUCA (volatile, uncertain, complex, and ambiguous) environment offers to those bold enough to step up. This book is what I wish I'd had back then. It's what I wish my parents and coaches had so we could have fully harnessed opportunities and turned small wins into bigger victories with unstoppable momentum and accelerated success.

I have now spent nearly two decades consulting and working in sports marketing and tech. I've collaborated with brands and teams to activate sponsorships, build fan experiences, manage large consumer platforms, and enhance customer engagement. This experience has given me a unique perspective on the evolution of brand partnerships, marketing, and

INTRODUCTION

collaboration at increasing scale. However, while valuable, this aspect of my career isn't the primary focus of my motivation for writing this book. Honestly, the most compelling reason comes from my role as a mom.

I have witnessed firsthand the critical gap in the conversation surrounding student athletes at this volatile time in college athletics, particularly in regard to their support systems. There's extensive discussion about the rights, potential earnings, and financial well-being of student athletes, but rarely does that discussion include their most significant supporters: their parents. Parents are the ones who plant and cultivate the seeds of their children's gifts and hold the shared vision for their future, yet they are often left out of key conversations and the decision-making process.

Yes, coaches, administrators, and consultants are all invested in developing student athletes to maximize their potential, but the role of parents is irreplaceable. As a parent, you must evolve to be the most effective leader for your children in this new stage of their lives so you can help enable their growth and development. To do that, you must pull up a seat at the table where you can partner with your children to navigate the ever-changing landscape.

While my primary focus is on parents, as I said, there will be plenty of applications in the chapters ahead for coaches, administrators, and consultants to steward new leadership, develop inner agility, and provide tools for success in their programs and work with young athletes. Quite frankly, we *all* have to step up. Our student athletes need us now more than ever.

I vividly remember a moment during my pregnancy with my triplet boys when I had to show up differently for my unborn team. My own world was changing at a rapid pace, to say the least. Fear, doubt, and worry had seeped into my thoughts, fueled by the medical risks associated with high-order multiples and my advanced maternal age. These external voices, though not malicious, were draining my energy, my focus, and my optimism, the precious resources my triplets needed to develop.

In that challenging time of uncertainty, I made a conscious decision to dump the negative thoughts and pump up the positive ones. My boys were counting on me, and I had to step into the role of the leader they needed. So I chose to improve myself and our circumstances by intentionally taking action. I chose to embrace the challenges and accept the fact that our new chapter as parents of triplets was going to be vastly different from anything I had known with our first child just a few years prior. That's when I turned a corner, and real growth began to happen—not on the outside, but on the inside. A switch was flipped, and I went on "offense" to show up as a leader for my little team. As a result, my boys were born healthier and stronger than the average triplets, a testament to the power of conscious effort, embracing uncertainty, and keeping a positive outlook.

Six years later, my boys are still growing, and so am I. Parenting is an ongoing journey, and I'm far from perfect. But the lessons learned are invaluable, and the key decision I made was to show up and embrace our unique path despite challenges and rapid changes. Raising triplets has been a different experience from raising my first child—one that has required far more creativity, flexibility, and adaptability.

As a parent-leader, I must grow with my children. To be my best for them, I must recommit to my own growth, purpose, and evolution. I'm a work in progress, even as I lead them through challenges and grow together with them.

INTRODUCTION

As a parent, you must understand that to truly support your children, you must also evolve. You can't stay stuck in old habits or beliefs about how things have always been done, whether in sports or life. The world is changing too fast to remain stagnant. Without committing to action and growth, you risk being left behind and missing out on your own potential and the acceleration of your young athlete's development.

This book is a call to action. I urge you, as a parent, to step up, focus, and make the conscious choice to face the challenges head-on. By doing so, you can guide your children through the murky waters of change and ensure they reach their full potential.

WINNERS AND SPINNERS

In times of rapid change, people tend to fall into two distinct categories: winners and spinners. Winners are the ones who charge ahead, take the initiative, and make decisive choices, ultimately landing in the winner's circle. On the other hand, spinners are the ones who get swept up in the whirlwind of accelerating change and challenges, which leaves them stuck in a perpetual cycle of indecision and inaction.

Those who have the courage to step up and lead can create a bold future for themselves and their children. I want to empower you to be among the winners by equipping you with the tools and mindset you need to navigate change effectively and seize opportunities.

As a former professional athlete, I understand the pressures and opportunities in competitive environments. As a consultant in sports marketing, I've witnessed the evolution of brand partnerships, the power of platforms, and collaborative engagement. And as a parent, I know the critical role parents play in their children's success and development.

By sharing these diverse experiences, I aim to provide you with a comprehensive understanding of how to tackle the rapidly changing landscape that lies ahead for you and your child athlete. In part 1, we're going to look at how you and your student athlete can navigate the rapidly changing environment of college athletics. And then, in part 2, we will explore the specific opportunities that are available in this new era of sports.

Spoiler alert: This isn't just about ensuring a winning season for your young athlete during their college years; this is about *your* winning season as well. After all, you're both on the home team.

PART ONE
THE CHANGING LANDSCAPE

CHAPTER ONE

VUCA (VOLATILE, UNCERTAIN, COMPLEX, AND AMBIGUOUS)

VUCA IS AN acronym that originated from military training scenarios. It stands for volatile, uncertain, complex, and ambiguous.[1] Soldiers are trained to operate successfully in environments that are evolving and unpredictable. This training aims to equip them with the skills to make better decisions, minimize risks, and lead their teams to successful mission outcomes, even in a rapidly changing environment. Today, the term VUCA has transcended its military roots and accurately describes our entire global environment.

The world we live in today is undeniably VUCA. Technological advancements are accelerating at an unprecedented pace, creating a surge of exponential growth in areas like artificial intelligence, machine learning, and blockchain technology. These advancements continually transform industries, causing disruption, volatility, and complexity as businesses scramble to stay ahead.

Globalization has added another layer to the VUCA environment. Our economies are more interconnected than ever before, both on the micro and macro levels. In many ways, this is a good thing. You can order diapers on Amazon and have them delivered within hours, thanks to local distribution centers connected to global corporations. However, this interconnectedness also means that decisions made in one country can have far-reaching impacts worldwide. A policy change in China or India can ripple through the entire global economy, affecting businesses and individuals in the United States and other places.

Political uncertainty and geopolitical instability further contribute to the VUCA landscape. Shifts in governments and institutions can impact regulations and supply chains. In 2021, for example, geopolitical instability led to significant delays in certain supply chains, with many people unable to obtain essential items. For example, garage doors became scarce, which delayed many home construction projects and inspections across the country.[2]

Inflation, recessions, and currency volatility make it difficult to predict and plan for the future. The rapid changes in economic conditions can make the ground feel unsteady, which only adds to the challenges of operating in a VUCA environment.

Our children are particularly affected by this VUCA world, especially in the realm of communication and social media. They face an accelerating barrage of information and a constant bombardment of messages from social media unlike anything previous generations experienced (or could even have imagined). They are growing up in a world where they are always "on," constantly pinged by social media and app notifications, text messages, and FOMO (fear of missing out) as they try to keep up with their always-on, ever-changing online presence. The pressure to stay connected can be overwhelming for them, particularly during developmental stages when social pressures are at their peak.

This phenomenon is particularly pronounced in the world of college sports, which epitomizes the VUCA environment more than just about anything else. And somehow, as parents, we have to help our children bear this mental load.

THE VUCA WORLD OF COLLEGE SPORTS

It's fair to say that the changing landscape of college sports these days is as VUCA as it gets. The pivotal moment of change occurred in July 2021 when NCAA rules changed, forever altering the landscape of college athletics. That was the date when restrictions on student athletes' ability to profit from their own personal brands—name, image, and likeness (NIL)—were lifted. The rapid rate of change in college sports has only accelerated since then, with legal and regulatory shifts that have utterly transformed the amateur nature of college sports. And we're seeing the effects in high school sports as well. On top of that, various states have enacted their own NIL laws, which have created a complex matrix of compliance requirements.

The good news is this new marketplace created immediate opportunities for athletes to capitalize on their reputation. The top one or two percent of athletes, the ones who are likely to go pro, quickly signed deals with brands and launched their own merchandise, enhancing their social media influence. Then came the collectives, entities that fundraise and negotiate deals with athletes to maintain competitive rosters, though they are not yet officially affiliated with schools. The relationship between universities, their boosters, and collectives that financially support NIL is expected to continue to rapidly evolve in 2025 and beyond.

Student athletes now have access to sponsorship deals, brand collaborations, partnerships, financial opportunities, and personal brand building, which allows for personal development and helps to build their entrepreneurial professional skills. In the past, most student athletes dedicated all of their time to sports, which left them with limited real-world experience upon graduation, but now they can engage in business activities, gain life skills, and build resumes alongside their athletic commitments.

The NIL opportunity has opened up a training ground for professional experiences, where career development, insights, and networking can occur that were previously denied to them. Similar to our generation's "first-job" accountability and learning, internships, and summer jobs—now athletes can bolster their resume and experience in preparation for life after college. Beyond the mere monetary benefits of name, image, and likeness opportunities, they also gain communication, marketing, financial planning, operational execution, partnership, and prioritization experience.

This is the upside of the recent changes, but this new landscape also presents numerous challenges. Notably, the lack of an official collective bargaining organization for student athletes means that each individual is responsible for navigating these opportunities alone. This places immense pressure on young athletes to make complex decisions that they previously didn't have to worry about.

VANQUISH VUCA WITH INNER AGILITY

The increasing rate of change in college sports is breaking down old structures and making traditional playbooks obsolete, which makes some parents say, "This isn't how it was done in my day." But here's the thing: There's no going back. Rather than ruminate about yesterday, the only way is to go forward. Changes like NIL aren't ruining college sports or compromising integrity. On the contrary, they are enhancing the student-athlete experience. That's the attitude we need to adopt.

To best equip our student athletes in this landscape, it's not enough to educate them about *what* to think about NIL. We need to equip them with *how* to think about the possibilities that this new NIL era has ushered in. It's not enough to take one course or lecture on NIL to see success. Setting your student athlete up for long-term success requires practice and a development process to build up a sustainable skill set that will continue to serve your athlete long after graduation.

Yes, there's still a lot to be done at the institutional and legislative levels in regard to NIL, but there are actions you and your student athletes can take right now to show up and accelerate your own goals that will maximize these opportunities. However, you have to move away from the twentieth-century "predict-and-plan" method of leadership and decision-making, which was risk-averse and based on historically accurate assumptions proven over time. That kind of decision-making process is now too slow and rigid to respond to these rapid changes and complexity.

The new twenty-first-century leadership model must embrace a "sense-and-respond" approach that acknowledges the presence of risk but treats it as an opportunity to rapidly learn and iterate. By sensing and responding to change, athletes can learn much faster and adapt more effectively as long as they can make sense of their environment and respond in real time.

A sense-and-respond approach requires our student athletes to develop inner agility. Fortunately, many of them already possess this ability on the field or court. A good athlete learns how to make quick decisions and adapt to dynamic situations in their respective sport, but now they need to apply that same adaptability to other areas of their lives.

The pillars of inner agility include the following:

- Adaptability
- Improved decision-making
- Resilience
- Creativity and innovation
- Stronger relationships

Enhanced adaptability means learning how to adjust strategies and behaviors in response to new information and changing circumstances. Increasing your self-awareness and how you process your thoughts, emotions, and reactions also lends a greater capacity for adaptability in the moment. More than ever, we must learn how to bend and flex in response to challenges.

The second pillar is **improved decision-making** based on sense-and-respond capabilities and discernment that enable you to see the invisible, hear what's going unsaid, and respond in action with imperfect information in a way that is aligned with your values and vision. Athletes with inner agility are better equipped to make informed and balanced decisions in the face of imperfect information and ambiguity. We will talk about this in-depth in a later chapter.

VUCA (VOLATILE, UNCERTAIN, COMPLEX, AND AMBIGUOUS)

The third pillar is **resilience**, particularly *emotional* resilience. Resilience is about maintaining your composure and recovering quickly from setbacks, managing stress, and maintaining a positive mindset. I come from a cheerleading background, and it's a little-known fact that in cheerleading competitions, teams are scored on their recoveries. If you can learn to maintain your composure under pressure, you can respond to real-time challenges effectively, but you must become better able to manage stress in the moment.

Additionally, inner agility fosters **creativity and innovation**. This is why some athletes can make unconventional plays, like a shortstop throwing the ball from behind their back or a soccer player making an incredible bicycle kick mid-air to score a goal. Their creativity allows them to find new ways to get the job done by experimenting and trying new things.

The final pillar of inner agility is **stronger relationships**. With self-awareness, empathy, and the recognition of other perspectives, you can build trust and communicate more effectively, which helps develop positive and developmental relationships with teams and stakeholders. With this mindset, feedback (even negative feedback) becomes an opportunity for improvement rather than mere criticism.

These five areas—**adaptability**, **improved decision-making**, **resilience**, **creativity and innovation**, and **stronger relationships**—are essential for developing inner agility because they enable both student athletes and their parents to better approach VUCA environments and lead through change. A comprehensive approach to developing inner agility and a growth-oriented mindset will set the foundation for success by teaching your student athlete to navigate the complexities of modern challenges, which will enable them to lead and excel in any environment long after they've left college behind.

However, the conversation around what it takes for an individual to be successful must evolve. It's not just about one person taking on the world but about enabling more people to join in and support the vision. We have to grow beyond the competitive environment we've come up in throughout our years in elite sports training and switch gears to the next level of collaboration. Think bigger about your impact and your future. You will only reach your maximum potential if your mission becomes about more than just you.

This starts with parents being the first to raise their hand and sponsor their children and embody the spirit of collective growth and support. It's our job to help our student athletes develop a growth-oriented mindset by showing them the way.

Building these skills will provide our student athletes with a platform that allows for continuous improvement, akin to automatic upgrades in the tech world. This, in turn, will help them win at every turn by continuously spiraling upwards. Like machine learning in AI, their platform must constantly evolve by incorporating feedback and becoming more effective over time.

We're going to look at exactly how you can begin to build this platform.

CHAPTER TWO

AGILITY FOR THE WIN

SUCCESS ISN'T JUST about sitting back and letting things happen—it's about getting out there and *making* things happen. Imagine you're in the final minutes of a game. Every play counts. You're on the balls of your feet, and you're 100 percent locked in, anticipating the developing play. Time slows down. You're mentally on offense, ready to make the next move, and you want the ball to come to you. No fear, just positive expectation and action orientation. You're ready to seize the opportunity and turn this intense challenge into a win. That's adaptive leadership in action. Adaptive leadership is your secret weapon, which is all about staying flexible, responsive, and innovative when the game changes unexpectedly.

This is as true for student athletes as it is for their parents. Your children need to lead with a mix of offense and adaptability, just as they do on the field. This means spotting and creatively responding to opportunities in this whirlwind phase of their lives. Sure, there will be setbacks—not every play leads to a touchdown—but that's where resilience comes in. They need to bounce back, stay strong under pressure, and keep moving forward.

We're not just talking about surviving or handling stress. They need to embrace a growth mindset—always aiming to get better, to learn from every experience, and push forward, no matter the score. Here's a winning formula to keep in mind:

$$(Action + Agility) \times (Growth\ Mindset + Resilience) = Long\text{-}Term\ Success$$

It all boils down to your (and their) mindset. This is the engine that drives your actions and attitudes and makes you a leader when others hesitate. Cultivate a mindset that's both positive and geared toward growth. Always try to look on the bright side and stay constructive, no matter what curveballs life throws at you—choose faith over fear and see challenges as opportunities, not just obstacles.

Now, you or your child might say, "Well, how can I do that? I'm a naturally pessimistic person," or, "I'm too much of a realist to always look on the bright side." But here's the thing: You can *build* a positive mindset with a bit of practice. Start by *intentionally* looking for the good in every situation, even when things don't go your way. Intentionally maintain an encouraging inner dialogue with yourself—become your own biggest cheerleader. And encourage your student athlete to do the same.

I'm not saying you should be unrealistically positive to the point of delusion. Instead, aim for a foundation of optimism that nudges you toward hope and constructive thinking, even during tough times. With this approach, you'll be ready to tackle anything that comes your way.

LEADERS ARE LEARNERS

Student athletes who get the most out of their college years tend to be the ones who eagerly dive into self-development and learning and view challenges as chances to grow rather than hurdles to dodge. They adopt a growth mindset of action and solutions, and they focus on progress, not perfection. They think of change as a thrilling adventure rather than a scary unknown. They choose faith and optimism over fear and discouragement, and they see new opportunities instead of closed doors.

So how do you see change? As a little exercise, take a look at the following phrase and say out loud what you see:

OPPORTUNITYISNOWHERE

You can look at this phrase in two very different ways, simply by putting spaces in different places. So, what did it say to you? It can say, "opportunity is nowhere," but with a slightly different perspective, it can instead say, "opportunity is now here." This little wordplay shows how your perception often shapes your reality. You and your student can *choose* to see opportunity in the chaos.

Start actively working on finding the good in every situation with a hopeful, optimistic outlook. Elements like gratitude, positive self-talk, stress management, and a solution-oriented approach all play a part. Even during peak stress, when everything seems to be falling apart, a positive mindset can help both parents and student athletes return to a baseline of optimism, ready to tackle the challenges head-on. You're literally raising the bar of your inner self-talk and positive expectations in your life.

Optimism lays the foundation for a growth mindset. If you can stay positive, even in the face of challenges, then you can focus on continuous improvement, taking action, seeking solutions, and turning challenges into opportunities for growth. With this mindset, success becomes more than a possibility—it becomes a near certainty, achieved through consistent effort and resilience.

WHAT IF...?

So practically speaking, how do you turn obstacles into opportunities and setbacks into success when you're operating in a VUCA environment? The secret ingredient is creativity. I know some folks, especially adults, might say, "But I'm not creative." Don't worry. This isn't about painting the Sistine Chapel. It's about sparking your natural curiosity. As humans, we're all inherently curious, which can lead to new perspectives and fresh ideas that fire up your creative mindset.

If you ever find yourself gripped by fear, doubting your abilities, or feeling left behind, just ask yourself, *What if...?* This simple question is like a key that unlocks the door to your curiosity and creativity. It lets you explore possibilities without the pressure of immediate action. Pondering different scenarios—What if my assumption isn't true? What if we responded like this or that? What could I be missing in this scenario?—helps you see how you might respond or act differently, which can help shift your mindset from fear to faith.

This is a perfect example of leading offensively instead of defensively. Picture a sailor on the seas in stormy weather, proactively anticipating changes in the wind, the next big wave to crash, and using the wind to adjust their sails from moment to moment. They go on offense, leaning into the storm and steering themselves into a clearing.

Compare that to a sailor who hunkers down, goes on defense, and their boat nearly gets bowled over with every crashing wave. They are directionless, at the mercy of each crashing wave that nearly capsizes them, spinning in circles inside the storm. They feel stuck and helpless in fear, waiting for the storm to pass and remaining purely reactive and unprepared to guide their ship through the storm. They're not chasing goals; they're dodging threats. And that is no way to create long-term success.

This idea goes beyond sports and applies broadly to the VUCA world we live in today and how you respond. Some people wait for things to return to "normal," stuck in a defensive stance, unwilling to accept that times have changed. Instead of creating a new path, they try to deal with whatever hits them next.

Let's use an example from the professional world to see how it applies to everyday leadership. Picture a young leader confidently presenting a vision for their department's future in a board meeting. They're proactive, steering the conversation and shaping the future. Contrast this with someone who comes to the meeting defensively, bracing for criticism. This person lets others dominate the discussion, playing defense and absorbing hits.

So whether you're on the field, in the boardroom, or navigating stormy seas, adopting a proactive, creative mindset makes all the difference. Even if you don't have all the answers up front, seize opportunities; don't just dodge problems. Ask, "What if...?" Spark your creativity in the face of change and challenges.

ADAPTIVE SKILLS ARE THE FUTURE

> *The future is already here—it's just
> not very evenly distributed.*
> —WILLIAM GIBSON

If you really want to help your student athlete now, as they are just about to step into this VUCA environment called college, focus on developing their adaptive skills. There are two types of skills they can learn during these years: **technical skills** and **adaptive skills**. Both are super important in a fast-changing world, but adaptive skills are the ones that will guarantee success, no matter the hurdles.

Again, to use a sports metaphor, you can teach a young athlete how to throw, catch, bunt, or steal bases. These technical skills are vital, of course, and high-performing college athletes usually excel at them. But technical skills can only take you so far. When athletes age out, exhaust their eligibility, or face physical limitations like worn-out knees, those technical skills alone won't keep them going. That's where adaptive skills come in—they're useful beyond the field and apply to every part of life.

Technical skills are specific to tasks and goals, and advancing your technical skills is referred to as horizontal development. Adaptive skills, however, are flexible and can be used in any situation. Learning and developing adaptive skills results in vertical growth, increasing the capacity to skillfully handle more as well as more complexity and uncertainty. In sports, a top athlete anticipates the play before the ball even reaches them. They know from experience that a certain swing will send the ball in a particular direction. They adapt to their changing environments because they can "see" opportunities that others don't yet, and they position themselves to make the winning plays.

This kind of quick thinking comes from intelligence, endless practice, and familiarity with the game, and it allows them to make fast, confident decisions. Consider Tom Brady. Whether or not you're a fan, there's no denying that his elite adaptive skills put him in the unique position to lead his teams to a record-breaking seven NFL Super Bowl rings. His multiple MVP titles and victories were due to his incredible agility, keen ability to read defensive formations, make quick decisions, and adjust his play calling to his advantage. Brady's ability to "see" developing plays and opportunities that even his elite opponents missed gave him a competitive edge and cemented his legacy as one of the greatest quarterbacks in NFL history.

Adaptive skills make athletes agile in any game situation, and these same skills are invaluable in life. **Emotional intelligence**, for example, is a key adaptive skill that includes self-awareness, self-regulation, social skills, and empathy, all of which allow people to connect well with themselves and others. Other essential adaptive skills are **resilience**, **self-direction**, and **leadership**, which enable student athletes to quickly learn and apply knowledge from different experiences to new challenges during college and long afterward.

Other important adaptive skills include **critical thinking**, **communication**, and **collaboration**. All of these adaptive skills are central to leadership development, but in today's VUCA world, **resilience** and **adaptability** are the true standouts for success. Your student athlete needs to prioritize developing these skills quickly because they're the best tools for navigating today's challenges.

EXAMPLES OF ADAPTIVE SKILLS

What does it mean to have adaptability? What skills make us more adaptive in VUCA situations and challenges?

- Resilience
- Emotional Intelligence
- Creative Thinking
- Critical Thinking
- Communication
- Collaboration
- Self-Direction and Leadership

In the past, technical skills were the golden ticket to moving up the corporate ladder, but things have changed. Nowadays, adaptive skills are the only path to ensure long-term success. Let's look at some eye-opening data from the World Economic Forum (WEF). Every four years, the WEF publishes a jobs report listing the top skills global companies crave. The 2023 report makes one thing clear: Adaptive skills are on the rise. The top skills these days are creative thinking, analytical thinking (basically critical thinking), technological literacy, curiosity and lifelong learning, resilience, flexibility, and agility. Notice most of them are related to adaptability.[3]

The WEF further predicts that, by 2030, the most important skills will be emotional intelligence, creativity, critical thinking, self-management, and making agile decisions in dynamic environments. This means now is the time to focus on adaptive skills, especially during these golden college years. College offers a unique environment full of support, learning opportunities, and a safe space for growth. It's the perfect time for your student athlete to dive in and soak up these skills because once they hit the workforce, their chances for reskilling or upskilling will be a lot harder to come by.

By jumping into developing their adaptive skills with both feet during college, your student can gear up for the future, armed with the adaptive skills they're going to need to thrive in the professional world. These skills will become their secret weapon for making smart decisions, being self-aware, and responding effectively to different situations. With these abilities, they can react in real time, rather than just following rigid plans and predictions. They will be able to make quick, effective decisions when it counts and explore new ideas and opportunities more readily.

So, yes, mastering technical skills like AI tools and new technologies is great, but remember: Tech tools come and go. Staying updated on the latest tools is important, but true success isn't about becoming a tech wizard. It's far more about honing your human abilities and inner agility. Focus on emotional intelligence, creativity, critical thinking, self-management, and adaptability. Your true value and success lie in developing what can be thought of as your own divinely inspired human operating system. This is as true for you as it is for your children. By powering up this internal system, you ensure your skills and abilities remain relevant no matter how the world changes.

Encourage your student athlete to develop their "humanness" and inner agility so they can operate at the next level and continuously upgrade their capabilities throughout life. This concept of a human operating system will become more apparent as we delve deeper into these ideas, but it all starts with the mindset that you model, encourage, and cultivate in your student athlete. This mindset is followed by taking intentional action to develop these adaptive skills.

CHAPTER THREE
RESILIENCE + GROWTH

IMAGINE PARENTS AND student athletes like superstar athletes on the same team, working together to develop a growth mindset and wielding the power of continuous improvement. A growth mindset isn't just a handy tool for navigating the future—it's the ultimate game changer. But what exactly does it mean to embrace a growth mindset?

Think of your mindset as a rookie athlete. It can't just sit on the bench and wait for the game to start; it needs training, attention, and regular practice. In a similar way, a growth mindset is all about making conscious choices in how you approach and respond to challenges. Forget the idea that you can just flip a switch or attend a single training camp and be set for the season. Mindset mastery isn't about quick fixes or instant victories; it's about consistent, daily workouts and regular practice. In other words, your mindset is a skill you can train and develop over time.

Start thinking of developing your mindset like training for a championship. What does this look like in practice? Chiefly, it means you begin intentionally aligning the simplest of your daily choices—how you act and react—with your grandest goals. You view each day as a new practice session, another chance to hone your skills and push your limits. Yes, there will be both victories and setbacks along the way, but every experience becomes part of the game.

Just as athletes constantly strive to improve, you, too, adopt a mindset of relentless pursuit, understanding that the effort itself is what builds your strength and resilience. So embrace the grind, the strategy sessions, and the thrill of progress, knowing that every step forward, no matter how small, brings you closer to your ultimate potential.

In a way, your mindset should operate like a high-performing sports team, which is always evolving and improving. Every thought should be directed (or redirected) toward the goal as you focus your mind on your growth journey. And just like winning athletes, a growth mindset is ever-expanding, always working hard to climb the ranks and advance. Over time, through intentional choices, you gain more skills and strategies, open up more opportunities, and build greater momentum toward your goal. Imagine the energy and drive of a team on a winning streak. That's what a growth mindset is like.

Of course, a winning team is made up of individual players, but they all operate as a cohesive unit, and in a similar way, a growth mindset is made up of different "players." We already named some of these players: optimism, emotional intelligence, adaptability, critical thinking, communication, collaboration, and leadership. Each of these players works together to support and enhance one another. As one player improves, they elevate the entire team's performance and strengthen the whole roster. So, for example, as you focus on being more optimistic, intentionally looking for the good in any situation, you also boost other players on your mindset team like creativity and adaptability.

At first, training this team might feel like running endless drills and laps. But as your capacity grows, each practice session becomes more productive. The point is this: You develop a growth mindset through intentional effort in how you choose to act and react to opportunities and challenges every single day. It doesn't happen by accident any more than a championship wrestling team wins a dual meet by accident. It comes from a deliberate effort to continuously improve as part of an ongoing journey of personal and professional development.

It is absolutely vital that your child works to develop a growth mindset during this critical time in their lives because the way they act and react to challenges and opportunities over the next four years is going to lay a foundation for the decades to come. And if you want to help them in this effort, then you need to model a growth mindset for them and encourage them to do the same. But you embrace a growth mindset for your own sake as well because, after all, you, too, have grand goals that you're working toward.

FEEDBACK IS FUEL

The more you train and develop a growth mindset, the more resilient you become, and resilience is like the ultimate superpower. Resilience is not just about bouncing back from setbacks—though that's definitely part of it. More than that, it helps you dance and maneuver through life's ever-changing challenges with grace.

Why do some people reach their full potential while others with so much promise fall short? *Feedback*. Those who shy away from feedback miss their chance to grow into their greatest potential. Every swing-and-miss for the batter is instant feedback. Every shot on goal that doesn't go in informs the next attempt. We hone our skills in action, and feedback is the fuel for growth. We don't grow without feedback. We can't process or practice resilience without setbacks. The iterative, bite-sized breakthroughs you gain by remaining in action will catapult you further and faster than any "lucky break."

Begin to think of each day as a series of exciting "what-if" experiments. Every choice you make becomes a chance to test new waters and discover what works best in a kind of playful experimentation. Instead of merely recovering from obstacles, you become nimble and open, ready to pivot and adapt as you encounter new situations. Further, any small wins or small failures from your experiments give you feedback to inform your next move. Resilience unlocks your brilliance.

Resilience is the cornerstone of continuous improvement. Every spin of the potter's wheel makes the masterpiece take shape. Have you ever heard the saying, "You don't get what you want—you get what you need"? That's the heart of resilience. Each experience—whether it feels like a win or a loss—teaches you something valuable and guides your next steps.

So what would this mindset look like in the life of your young student athlete? Let's make it real.

For me, this lesson got *very* real at the ripe old age of eleven years old. I was the starting pitcher in the twelve-and-under fast-pitch PONY League World Series in Papillion, Nebraska (I won't say what year, but let's just say Madonna was crushing it on MTV at the time). After a great tournament, it all came down to the final game to win the National Championship title. There was a lot of pressure to perform, to say the least. It had been a long season, and our little team from Flossmoor,

Illinois, was ready to take on the team from Chino Hills, California, for the win.

Being in the moment, every pitch was a challenge, the dynamic game environment, the heightened sense that each pitch mattered. Fortunately, throughout that season, my dad instilled in me a one-word lesson: "stick-to-itiveness." As a budding pitcher, the umpires didn't always call it as I saw it, but I couldn't dwell on the past. With so many repetitions on the mound, I had more opportunities than any other player on my team to practice resilience. I had to let the momentary flushed cheeks and heat under my collar subside when the umpire called a ball that was clearly (in my view) a strike and go on to the very next pitch.

Every pitch, every play, every developing defensive motion behind me—I couldn't let the mistakes weigh me down. I had to let them inform my next move. The feedback from those umpires was fuel, for sure. It fired me up to be *that* much better on the next pitch, to win the "battle" with each hitter I faced. Ultimately, I was tweaking and adjusting my strategy and my approach every time. I couldn't let a batter getting a hit off me deter my ability to square up against the very next batter. Stick-to-itiveness: no matter what came our way.

Now, to be honest, we did *not* come away with the title. So, yes, this advice is coming from the runner-up World Series pitcher (two years in a row), but the lessons in resilience, the reps on the mound that let me elevate my mental game with each pitch, were invaluable for adapting to the changing landscape we find ourselves in today (and have been in for a while, frankly). With resilience, you're not just keeping up with the world—you're thriving amid change, leading, and continually unlocking your potential, and embracing new opportunities for improvement at every turn.

With resilience, you and your child can effectively shed the emotional baggage of failure and move forward with a fresh and more informed perspective. Even the most resilient leaders aren't immune to disappointment. Life is full of struggles, challenges, and unforeseen letdowns. Negative emotions are part of our human processing system, and resilience comes from an empowered way of processing that negative emotion. It's not the dismissing of disappointment; it's absorbing and choosing to find the opportunity in it. You intentionally think of failure not as a permanent defeat but as a treasure chest of new insights.

Do you see why this is so powerful, especially in a VUCA environment? As you navigate life's shifting terrain, resilience keeps you on your toes and helps you adapt quickly and effectively.

With resilience, you don't just weather the change—you excel amid evolution, steadily access your potential, and embrace development opportunities with each new challenge.

ENJOYING EVERY PLAY

Think of a growth mindset as your ultimate game plan for success. You're not just sprinting toward the finish line; you're enjoying every play in the game of learning. This winning strategy was first introduced by psychologist Carol Dweck in the late '70s and early '80s. Dweck's research revealed that hard work and practice often produce better results and more wins than innate talent.[4]

People tend to think that only those with natural talent win, but Dweck's findings showed that with consistent effort, almost anyone can clinch a victory. Of course, this isn't limited to sports but applies to every field and every part of life. If you will intentionally build perseverance, learn to bounce back from setbacks, and stay agile, you are far more likely to succeed in life.

Another word for this attitude is "stick-to-itiveness." Dad knew what he was talking about. Again, you can train yourself to do this. Your student athlete can develop stick-to-itiveness. They already do it on the field, don't they? High-performing athletes cherish training sessions and practice drills; they don't just celebrate the scoreboard. They like to learn from unexpected fumbles and improve so they can prepare for the next play. You just have to apply that same on-the-field mindset to the rest of life.

To do this, you have to intentionally picture adversity not as a penalty but as a chance to reset and strategize. You have to treat challenges as opportunities for growth. At first, this might be difficult, especially when facing a big setback, but over time, it makes you more resilient, just like repeated practice and learning on the field creates a stronger player. And as a parent, as you become more resilient, you become more able to help your child athlete through their own tough game, just like a great coach.

Resilience requires resistance to grow. The resistance in the challenge feels like tension, but it is bringing forth a powerful force that will slingshot you forward toward new heights if you harness it.

Repeat it like a mantra: Every setback is just another chance to score big.

CHAPTER FOUR

TRANSITIONS

ONE OF THE most difficult things for a parent to deal with during this dramatic time period in their child's life is the changing nature of their relationship to their child. Many struggle to embrace the change, and some even refuse to see it. They continue trying to parent, make decisions, and lead their children the same way even as they move into adulthood and transition into college life. Unfortunately, the old approach becomes increasingly ineffective, and parents who don't make the change often find themselves getting pushed out as their child embraces new mentors and influences in their lives.

I want to help you make a strong transition as a parent so you can continue to be an important guiding force in your child's life during the college years, but you have to embrace the change. Part of what makes this so difficult is that your children are going through a profound life transformation at the same time as you are going through a transformation, and both of you have to embrace the change. That takes courage.

Remember: As a parent, you're not just helping your children step into their own potential and greatness; you are also stepping into your own potential and greatness. You are both embarking on a new journey together, though you're moving toward different goals. And on this journey, as a parent, your role is a bit like the role of Yoda toward Luke Skywalker. You become an advisor and role model for your young Skywalker so they can set off into the galaxy, ready to make wise decisions and create their future in this new landscape.

But you are no longer making the decisions for them. And that is the hard part, isn't it? Yoda doesn't go with Luke. He shares wisdom, advises him, provides some important lessons, and then lets Luke go off and make decisions for himself. Quite frankly, Yoda doesn't like all of the decisions Luke makes, but he doesn't stop him from doing so. He doesn't step in and try to overrule him. Why? Because he knows this is a necessary transition in Luke's training. Luke must take all of the wisdom and lessons he has received, and he must now go off and figure out how to apply them.

This is exactly what happened with my dad and me. After my sophomore year of high school, I was burned out from ten years of year-round competitive fast-pitch softball, but I didn't lose my edge to keep growing. I decided that I would focus on coed cheer and stunt exclusively during my junior and senior years of high school.

It was a heart-wrenching realization for my dad because he knew that by choosing to end my softball career after my sophomore year, I was also ending the familiar father-daughter bonding ritual we'd had through the years. I knew it was the right thing for me. My dad wasn't so sure at the time, but he supported my decision nonetheless.

I'm sure he had visions of potential college softball scholarships, teams, and my accumulated elite player skills all going out the window with that decision. It was a hard pill to swallow for a father and his sixteen-year-old daughter, but it was a decision I made to stay true to myself. When I finally hung up the cleats once and for all, it was hard on our relationship for a short while, but after the initial "falling out" over our shared vision for my Varsity athletics goals, my father still kept showing up and supporting my decision to go exclusively into competitive cheer and stunt on my high school coed team.

Even though he didn't know a High V from a Basket Toss, he cheered me on at every competition. In my senior year, my Oakmont High School coed cheer and stunt squad won the United Spirit Association (USA) National Championship with a routine that I choreographed. It was a pivotal moment. I recall catching a glimpse of the "proud-father" smile on his face as he helped me lift the huge trophy. Dad didn't see that one coming when I quit playing softball, but he teared up too. He was part of my "home team," and we won. We were a team. Always will be.

He couldn't tell me what moves to do, but he could show me what real support and leadership look like as a parent. Together, both he and my mom remained steadfast, invested, and committed to supporting my goals during a major pivot from competing on the field to the stage.

It's tough, parents. Embracing this change in your relationship with your own child is never easy, but it's necessary. I now see that courage in my dad's response to change, and I appreciate his "Yoda" support that much more today. What makes it even harder these days is that the college environment, and college athletics in particular, has changed and continues to change. If you cling to "the way we've always done it" or lament, "This is not how things were done when I was in college," then you may become more of a hindrance than a help.

Yes, you want to share all of your knowledge and wisdom with your child, but you can't let your own growth stagnate by holding onto outdated practices. The galaxy is ever-changing, and so must you be. Luke will never become a Jedi if Yoda is unwilling to step back and let him lead.

FACING THE STORM

If you want to continue to be an effective leader in the life of your child, then you must commit to your own journey of change, learning alongside your young Skywalker while helping foster an environment where both of you can grow and thrive. But that's going to require you to let go of the past, embrace the present, and boldly step into a changing future. And may the Force be with you.

No wonder so many parents struggle during this phase of their child's life. Quite frankly, we have it harder than Yoda did. He didn't have to deal with the constant buzz of cell phones, the endless stream of emails, or the 24/7 demands of our digital lives. He didn't have to worry about Luke's college shenanigans ending up on the internet.

Thank goodness there weren't cell phones or social media when we were in college. We got to make our mistakes in relative privacy, away from the scrutinizing eyes of the digital world. Let's be honest: Even those of us who were "good kids" still made some questionable decisions, but they remained in the past, untethered from the permanent record of the online universe.

Today's kids are on a similar journey of growth but with the added pressure of always being "on." VUCA is their daily reality, and it's amplified by another acronym: FOMO. The fear of missing out is made all the worse thanks to technology, as our children are constantly bombarded with information, social pressures, and the stress of geopolitical and economic uncertainties. As a result, many young people today are unsure if they'll ever achieve what was once considered the American dream, like owning a home. They're dealing with a relentless flood of information and social pressure that we never had to face at their age. When everything feels so precarious, it becomes much harder to perceive and make the most of the opportunities that lie ahead.

Parents, we're in this new territory too. The endless Slack messages, the work emails you feel compelled to answer even on a Sunday night—these are all signs of a new world that demands our attention around the clock. It can feel like everyone and everything wants a slice of your energy and attention all the time. Add to that the uncertainty in the macroeconomic landscape, and it's no wonder the mental load feels heavier than ever before.

If you're experiencing this strain, imagine how it must be for your kids. As parents, we generally have a larger capacity to deal with stress, but young, developing students are still building their resilience. The constant stress and pressure can easily divert them from their best path. It is incredibly difficult to stay focused and on track.

So, what do we do? Again, we channel our inner Yoda. We guide, we support, and we set an example. We acknowledge that the mental load is real and that it affects all of us. We show our children how to navigate the VUCA storm, not by shielding them from it but by equipping them with the tools and mindset to handle it. We teach them to take a breath, to find their center amidst the chaos, and to embrace the journey with courage and resilience.

This acronym is a helpful tool to remind you of what you can do to facilitate a strong transition for your athlete and for yourself at this crucial time:

GUIDE

- **G — Growth:** Encourage them to adopt a growth mindset for continuous learning and stay involved in environments that support their character development.
- **U — Understanding:** Know the landscape and understand the rules (legal and compliance) as it pertains to your athlete's unique situation. Cultivate empathy and a deep understanding of your child's unique path.
- **I — Integrity:** Emphasize trustworthiness and ethical decisions that align with core values. Most importantly, show up as the role model of these values so your child can witness you in action.
- **D — Direction:** Provide a clear vision and guidance, helping them stay focused on long-term goals.
- **E — Empowerment:** Build up confidence by supporting their self-belief, independence, and ownership mindset.

Remember: The Force is strong within all of us. You'll work alongside your athlete as a guide, but ultimately let them decide. By embracing the challenges together, we can help our young Skywalkers navigate this new world and emerge stronger, wiser, and ready to take on whatever comes their way.

WHAT'S NEXT FOR YODA?

As your young Jedi takes their first steps into the galaxy of college life, you might find yourself facing your own monumental shift. You've spent years dedicating yourself to your child's growth and success. You've sacrificed weekends, sat in the bleachers for every ball game, and committed to after-school activities, camps, and recruitment events. Now, your young Skywalker is ready to embark on their next chapter, and you're left pondering, "What's next for me?"

While your child is learning to navigate their new world, you're also coming face-to-face with shifts in your own life. Suddenly, you have more time on your hands. You find yourself reevaluating your friendships and perhaps even questioning if your marriage is the same as it was before the whirlwind of competitive sports took over.

Some uncertainty is understandable. With the spotlight now turning back to you, it's time to dust off the cobwebs in areas of your life that have been sidelined. Maybe you've been too busy as the parent of a competitive athlete to address certain aspects of your own identity. And now, with more time to focus on yourself, you might wonder, *Who am I without the constant hustle and bustle of supporting my child?*

This period of transition requires courage—the courage to look in the mirror and acknowledge that you aren't the same person you were before having kids. You're likely not the same person you were before your child became a competitive athlete and demanded so much of your time, attention, and resources. You have evolved. The question is, do you have the courage to step into this next phase of your life and embrace the possibilities? Remember: Change isn't the *problem*—it's the *possibility*.

Reimagining your identity is no small feat. How can you begin to redefine who you are and how you show up for yourself? By exploring new interests, rekindling old passions, and investing in your personal growth. You now have a chance to rediscover what makes you tick outside of being a parent. So embrace this opportunity and take some time to reflect on your own journey. Celebrate the accomplishments of raising a child who is ready to take on the world, and look forward to your own exciting adventures ahead.

As you stand on the doorstep of this exciting new phase of your own life, remember that—just like your child—you, too, have to step into the unknown with confidence, embrace your evolving identity, and find joy in the process. Fortunately, you've navigated plenty of challenges before, and this is just another chapter in your own ever-unfolding story. Remember: **Modern leaders *grow* through challenges—they don't just *go* through challenges.** As parents, we lead the way by showing up to grow through our own transitions so that our children can grow through theirs.

HANDING OVER THE KEYS

To use a slightly different metaphor, up to this point in your child's life, you've been behind the wheel, both literally and figuratively. You've been guiding them on their journey to elite athletics. You've been the driver, making all the critical decisions, booking the hotels, and finding the right coaches and trainers. But now, as your child enters college, it's time to hand over the keys and transition from driver to passenger.

There's a concept that's useful in coaching teams toward a shared goal. It's called DACI, which stands for Drivers,

Approvers, Contributors, and Informed. Though DACI is typically used for managing projects, it's equally effective in helping parents understand their evolving role with their college-age kids. When your goal was to advance your child into collegiate athletics, you were undoubtedly the Driver, steering every decision and making sure everything was in place for their success.

As the Driver, you have been orchestrating every move, from registration forms to reaching out to recruiting coaches. And your child, ideally, has been the Approver, excited and committed to the journey. But now, it's time for a fundamental shift in these roles. Your child is stepping into the Driver's seat and taking control of their life and their vision.

As they transition into this role, you must switch seats in the vehicle and become a parent partner. Becoming a parent partner means supporting them without steering the car. It's not an easy change to make, but your child needs to take the lead. It is their time now to drive not only their performance on the field but also their broader life vision. When you willingly hand over the keys, it shows that you trust their ability to navigate their path, and that's going to be a powerful motivator for them.

The reality is, in this new dynamic, you might find yourself moving out from a Driver role or even an Approver role to that of a Contributor or an Informed supporter. The Approvers will probably be coaches, compliance officers, or the institutional bodies that make sure your child meets all necessary standards and commitments. Your role, then, is to contribute your wisdom, experience, and unwavering support and show up as a model of resilience and adaptability.

Just as Yoda didn't pilot Luke's X-wing, you shouldn't try to micromanage your child's journey. Instead, provide guidance and let them learn to maneuver through life's challenges on their own. Otherwise, they will not develop the mindset or the adaptive skills they need to achieve their long-term goals in life. This is their time to step up and act like an owner. Specifically, encourage them to develop and take ownership of four areas to stay on a winning path:

- Vision for Their Future
- Athletic Ability
- Reputation
- Platform

In the coming chapters, we'll show you how to enable your athlete to develop their ownership in these key areas, alongside their adaptive skill set.

As they step up to lead themselves and make their own decisions, it doesn't mean you have to step back completely. Rather, you are shifting your focus. As I said, you still play a crucial role in their success story as a Contributor by serving as a steadfast supporter and role model. Other contributors will also come into play—private coaches, performance advisors, recruiting professionals, even marketing or legal counselors—all aligned to accelerate your child's development. This is where programs and resources like this book come in handy, offering tools to help you become an effective parent partner so you're not left on the side of the road as your child speeds towards their future.

Even if you're not "coaching" on their little league sidelines anymore, you can still contribute to their continued growth in new, meaningful ways by ensuring they have an evolved relationship with you, showing up and leading in your own new chapters, and investing in deliberately developmental environments for them to build their character and agility.

Support them without overshadowing their journey. A lot of parents struggle with the emotional weight of handing over the keys. Even Yoda had an emotional struggle when Luke flew off in his X-wing. It's a big change, but I strongly encourage you to embrace this new chapter with enthusiasm. As a matter of fact, no one—not a mentor, coach, boss, manager, or college sweetheart—will replace the leader they have in you as their parent. You're not losing your place in their life—you're enhancing it by empowering them to take control as they head off into the vast, exciting galaxy.

PART TWO
BUILDING A PLATFORM FOR ULTIMATE SUCCESS

CHAPTER FIVE

THE POWER OF A PLATFORM

IF YOU REALLY want to empower your child athlete's massive potential, then you need to help them build a platform they can use as a foundation for all the activities that will contribute to their success. And while you're at it, you need to build your own platform as a parent.

What do I mean by a "platform"? That's a good question, and understanding this concept is going to be incredibly important. There are two ways to think about platforms. Let's look at both.

First, a platform is defined as "a base or foundation that supports other structures or activities." Every word in that definition is important. Imagine a physical platform, like a stage. It elevates you and gives you the standing to address and serve others. Now think about a platform as a set of principles or values that define who you are and what you stand for.

Second, a platform is also something that serves as leverage for *others* to stand on or plug into. In this sense, think of a platform as a service that is designed to accelerate or elevate other people. A powerful platform can sustain entire ecosystems, delivering value for everyone it supports and creating a massive positive impact.

During this next stage of your and your child's lives, it is going to be incredibly important to build a platform for *their* success and for *your* success in the years ahead. So let's start with your platform because it's entirely possible that you've been so focused on your child's success that you haven't even considered your own success in the years ahead.

You're in a period of transition, but you can *choose* to courageously step forward and recommit to your own growth through the challenges ahead. So what does it mean for a parent to build their own platform for success?

First and foremost, get clear on what you stand for—your values and principles. These are the rock-solid pillars that prop up your platform. Without pillars, platforms crumble. Remember: Even as an adult, your child will continue to refer to, reference, and look to you as an example. Your values and principles guide your decision-making, provide an example for your child, and they also allow you to elevate others. So get crystal clear on your values, stay committed to your growth, and watch how your platform supports and inspires the people around you.

YOUR LIFE OPERATING SYSTEM

Ultimately, the goal is to keep building yourself up. Think of it as creating the blueprint for living your most purpose-filled life—a "life operating system" guided by your core values and principles. This system not only shapes your path but also strengthens your foundation so you can support your child more effectively. As they build their own platform, your understanding of these concepts will make you an invaluable partner, able to guide, support, and share insights that empower them on and off the field.

When you have a strong foundation to stand on, you're better equipped to handle the mental load. You'll be more present, manage stress effectively, and avoid getting caught in cycles of negative thoughts or unproductive habits. In showing your child the value of a steady foundation, you're also reinforcing the importance of structure, purpose, and resilience.

It's okay not to have all the answers. Embracing this mindset can be empowering. Approach life with the enthusiasm and curiosity of a rookie: ready to learn, open to change, and excited about tackling new challenges. Rookies may not know everything, but their openness and willingness to dive in make them unstoppable—and modeling this mindset will show your child how powerful a growth-focused outlook can be.

Surround yourself with like-minded individuals who lift you up and reinforce your commitment to both your child's and your own platforms. Share your setbacks and victories with a supportive network. This journey isn't meant to be traveled alone, and creating a strong support system benefits both you and your child.

In this new chapter of life, you're transitioning from being the driver in your child's life to becoming a true partner in their journey. You've been their rock, cheering from the sidelines, guiding them through the challenges of competitive sports. Now, as they venture out to build their platform, it's your time to shine too. By deepening your understanding of these platform-building principles, you're able to give them the best support while also creating your own "winning season" with renewed goals, interests, and dreams.

Set goals, explore your passions, and invest in your personal growth. Just as your child is growing and reaching new heights, so should you. Dust off those dreams you tucked away and bring them to the forefront. This is your chance to bravely recommit to your own potential, applying the same platform-building framework that will help your child excel. Not only will you be a stronger partner to them, but you'll also reignite the path to your own greatness.

SETTING A STRONG FOUNDATION FOR YOUR PLATFORM

Building your platform as a parent of a college athlete is about establishing a foundation built on trust, a long-term outlook, strategic decision-making, and creating meaningful value within your ecosystem. Here's how to embrace these principles in a way that strengthens both you and your family's journey:

First, reflect on your interests and goals. **Seek clarity on a purpose-driven vision**—this becomes your North Star, guiding strategic decisions and partnerships and creating accelerated value if you're aligned with this vision. Take the time to consider what truly excites you—those dreams, hobbies, or business ideas that bring both passion and purpose to your life. Evaluate each interest through the lens of trust: trust in yourself to pursue these goals and confidence that they align with your values and strengths. Write down your interests, goals, and dreams, no matter how big or small. This reflection process helps build a foundation for long-term commitment and growth.

A winning season for you is about finding balance and fulfillment, creating personal victories that run alongside those of your child. Picture yourself thriving—engaged in pursuits that matter to you, achieving your milestones, and feeling a deep sense of accomplishment. This season is not only marked by your achievements but also by your ability to adapt, grow, and find joy in the journey.

Remember: You are a role model for your child. By investing in your own platform, you demonstrate the lifelong journey of growth, resilience, and value creation. Embrace this chapter with enthusiasm, understanding that change brings opportunities for transformation. Show up for yourself with the same dedication you've shown for others, and let this winning season be defined by the impact you make on your terms.

UNLOCKING YOUR ATHLETE'S POTENTIAL

As a parent, you already know how important it is to show up for your kids. But why is building a platform necessary for your student athlete's journey? Well, the purpose of a platform is to fast-track their short-term gains without sacrificing their integrity or long-term impact.

Think of a platform as a springboard that will help them leap toward better opportunities, greater visibility, and an expanded support system. Some of the benefits of building a platform are for here and now, but you're also setting them up for lasting success long after the college years.

In a literal sense, a platform is a raised level surface that they can stand on in order to get a broad perspective of their surroundings. They will be able to look beyond the "front row" into a landscape full of opportunities that they might not otherwise know were there. But you have to focus on creating a sustainable platform built of solid principles and practices so it can guide their long-term vision and gains.

A well-built platform increases influence, impact, and even income. It's a holistic approach to long-term success. It also gives your child a consistent set of instructions on how to show up, a game plan to guide their actions so they know what needs to be done day by day to build momentum toward their dreams and goals. And it helps them set those goals as well. After all, you need a clear definition of success before you can work toward achieving it.

On this journey, the prize isn't just about winning games but winning at life. It's about seeing your children materialize their potential, gain confidence, and become the best version of themselves. As a parent, isn't that the ultimate reward for all of your hard work? Don't we want them to flourish and bloom and become the champions we always knew they could be? So, embrace this exciting journey with your child. Understand that building a platform is about setting them up for a lifetime of success with the same dedication and passion you've shown all along.

And remember: A platform isn't a static thing; it's dynamic and ever-evolving. Think of it as a living, breathing entity that grows and adapts with you and your child over time. There's always room for growth and new opportunities. You're building a platform and life operating system that is personalized and sustainable because it's adaptable to change.

To use another metaphor, you can visualize a bridge. A good bridge is designed to be sturdy, with a stable base and strong pillars to hold it up. At the same time, it must also be able to bend and flex so it can withstand high winds, storms, and even earthquakes. But ultimately, the purpose of the bridge is to provide a platform that allows you and other people to get where they want to go. And if you own the bridge, then you get to choose who has access to it.

The same goes for your child's platform. It must be solid at the base, composed of firm values and principles, but flexible enough to handle challenges and changes in the environment. And just as some bridges are designed for different kinds of vehicles (cars versus trains versus pedestrians), your child's platform needs to be personalized and sustainable.

And as they get valuable feedback on their bridge, they can make improvements to strengthen the base, make it more flexible, and so on—that's continuous learning. Over time, it becomes even more effective at propelling them and others far in their lives.

So, building a platform is about thoughtful planning and continuous evolution. It's about creating a sturdy base and flexible bridge that is always ready to move them forward. The key is to embrace the journey, keep improving, and watch as the platform helps you and your student athlete soar.

Having said all of that, I'm now going to take you step-by-step through the process of building a platform for your child's success, as well as your own.

COLLABORATION IS THE WINNERS' EDGE

I recommend an approach that I refer to as a "PLATFORMULA" because it is both a platform and a formula that a student athlete can use to build their NIL (name, image, and likeness) personal brand and business the right way from the get-go. I've created this methodology to help students and their parents spot opportunities, train for the prize, master the right mindset, and develop essential skills that will enable them to make a lasting impact. Training for the prize means building the capacity and character to be a leader but also training to become professional so they can succeed with NIL activities and any other entrepreneurial endeavors in the marketplace.

Unlike cookie-cutter playbooks, the PLATFORMULA is tailored to your child. Ultimately, it's about discovering what sets them apart, understanding their purpose and mission, and building a platform around that. Think of it as an agile method that evolves with them and allows their full potential to shine through their personal brand, reputation, and activities.

Remember: They only have a short window of time to leverage their NIL in college. By following the PLATFORMULA, they can avoid costly mistakes, dodge pitfalls, and stay on track to create an asset that will serve them for years to come. This isn't just about their personal success either; it's about professional excellence and fulfilling their life's purpose. Who wouldn't want to jump on that opportunity?

Think of their personal brand as the number one business asset. But remember: Your personal brand isn't about *you*. It's about who you serve. We rise to our full potential by lifting others. I am simply helping them develop the skills they need to build, maintain, and serve at the highest level, all in a sustainable, flexible, and service-oriented way. By applying agile methodology, your child builds their platform, belongs to a supportive ecosystem, and becomes a leader with a growth-oriented mindset. Curating their personal brand and leveraging their name, image, and likeness are just the beginning.

Now, let me be real: The scope of what we're going to cover over the next few chapters is broad and extensive, but you're not going to try to "boil the ocean" all at once. Instead, I recommend a phased approach where you support the growth of your student athlete at their own pace. Yes, college is a limited window of time in their lives, but they still have to work through their roadmap, goals, behaviors, and discoveries at a speed that suits them. Long-term success is not built overnight, but we can jumpstart the process.

Think of it as a "do-it-with-me" evolution of learning and applying. You don't want to overwhelm your student athlete with big life questions before they've even had a chance to knock on a door and ask for a deal. Instead, the purpose is to provide context for their decisions and a clear path forward. For the Yodas, it's about imparting wisdom and guiding from a place of experience. For the Luke Skywalkers, it's about harnessing that rookie energy and eagerness to learn.

So, the PLATFORMULA isn't just a framework—it's a journey. A journey where you and your student athlete evolve together, learning, applying, and growing every step of the way. With that in mind, let's dive in.

CHAPTER SIX

THE REAL NIL OPPORTUNITY

*It's not about the paper chasing,
it's about the purpose chasing.*
—MIKE TODD

ONE OF THE most significant changes in college athletics that has occurred in recent years was the new NCAA ruling introduced in 2021 that said college athletes can now make money from the commercial use of their name, image, and likeness (NIL). But in this chapter, I want to highlight the real NIL opportunity, which goes beyond the buzz about monetary benefits.

We're going to explore the reality of NIL versus the common expectations people have. Most of the headlines focus on the financial side of NIL, but the true value of NIL extends far beyond money. In fact, the monetary side often becomes the secondary benefit—the outcome of something much deeper.

The real juice, the part that's truly worth squeezing, comes from the learning, growth, and long-term success that go hand in hand with NIL activities. That's because NIL provides student athletes with a whole host of opportunities that help them develop business skills, foster entrepreneurship, and build personal brands that can carry them far beyond their athletic careers.

Let's start by taking a good, hard look at what NIL is. NIL stands for name, image, and likeness, which refers to three key elements that athletes have the right to profit from in commercial endeavors. At its core, NIL is about the right of publicity, a legal concept that protects an individual's ability to control the commercial use of their identity. Prior to 2021, student athletes were not permitted by the NCAA to use their NIL for commercial activities. Other college students, like artists, musicians, business majors, and even spirit squads who weren't under the NCAA athletic restrictions, have been using their NIL for entrepreneurial and commercial activities without penalty.

However, when the NCAA's rules changed, they lifted restrictions that used to prevent college athletes from leveraging their own NIL for financial gain. Essentially, the NCAA had been suppressing athletes' right of publicity, and this change recognized that athletes deserve to have this right respected. Initially, the NCAA called this change an "interim" policy, but recently, they removed that label without making any significant changes. So, now it is simply their official policy, and the NCAA continues to deal with the repercussions and further litigation settlements as a result of this historic ruling.

Let's suppose an athlete's photo is taken while they are wearing a certain athletic brand, and the brand uses that image for promotional purposes without the athlete's consent. That would be a violation of the athlete's right of publicity because no contract was established for the use of their NIL. But NIL is not just about protection. It's also about the *proactive* opportunity for athletes to leverage their brand by turning their names, images, and likenesses into real assets.

LEVERAGING THE NEW NIL LANDSCAPE

There are three main points to the NCAA's new policy. **First**, athletes can now engage in NIL activities as long as they follow the policies of their institution and the laws of the state where their school is located. **Second**, college athletes in states that haven't yet passed NIL laws can still participate in NIL without fear of repercussions, as NCAA guidelines broadly permit NIL involvement, subject to institutional policies. Most states are catching up quickly, with roughly thirty-nine out of fifty-one states and territories having passed or proposed NIL laws as I write this. Most of those states have allowed high school athletes to also participate in NIL activities within their state's specific guidelines. The trend is clear: It's only a matter of time before this is universal. **Third**, athletes are allowed to seek professional service providers to help manage their NIL activities.

Of course, student athletes must be compliant with their state laws, as well as the specific rules of their school and conference, to ensure their participation in NIL doesn't jeopardize their status. While the NCAA has opened the door, the responsibility now rests with the athletes to understand and navigate the matrix of rules that govern their particular situations. So the opportunity is there for them to seize, but it requires diligence, understanding, and a proactive approach.

So let's speak a little more concretely. Let's look at some specific examples of NIL activities that student athletes are engaging in today. The opportunities are vast and range from traditional methods of earning money to more entrepreneurial ventures. For example, athletes can now be paid for endorsements, signing autographs, selling memorabilia, running their own camps and clinics, or making personal appearances. They can also earn income from merchandise featuring their name or image, and through roles such as affiliate marketers, brand ambassadors, or through referral marketing.

Some emerging areas of NIL include licensing the use of digital likenesses in video games and other emerging technology like NFTs, which are essentially digital collectibles, as a form of modern-day trading cards. While only top-tier athletes typically venture into NFTs, it's still a growing field of opportunity. Beyond that, athletes can get paid for a variety of entrepreneurial activities such as blogging, podcasting, public speaking, product creation, book authorship, or even producing their own original music or artwork.

To be clear, the majority of NIL deals at the moment tend to revolve around social media, where athletes collaborate with brands to create content for online promotions, but social media is only one aspect of the NIL landscape. Don't assume that NIL opportunities are only for athletes interested in social media. That couldn't be further from the truth. The breadth of NIL opportunities extends well beyond social media and offers a range of ways for student athletes to build a platform and earn income.

BEYOND THE HEADLINES

Since 2021, the media has focused on flashy stories about athletes securing seven-figure NIL deals, posing in front of luxury cars, or signing contracts with major brands. The media generally plays up the most dramatic stories because, of course, they rely on viewership, clicks, and interest for their own businesses. But these sensationalized headlines fail to paint the full picture of what NIL truly offers.

THE REAL NIL OPPORTUNITY

In reality, **NIL is the single greatest leadership development opportunity of our time**, and its true merit goes far beyond monetary gain. The glitz and glamor that dominate the headlines are merely distractions from the real value NIL brings. NIL is more akin to on-the-job learning, similar to your first job or internship while in college. It's experiential, fast-paced, and entrepreneurial, and it gives student athletes a chance to develop real-world skills that create a snowball effect of momentum and opportunity. Yes, these opportunities can lead to financial success, but their true value lies in the learning and growth they foster.

The headlines often focus on collectives, high-dollar recruiting deals, and transfer portal disputes. If you do some cursory research, you'll read stories about the largest universities, conferences, and what the NCAA or state governing bodies are planning. The media covers Title IX concerns, legal issues, big brands, and marketing partners entering the NIL space. They regularly discuss agents, professional service providers, and mass marketing platforms. But student athletes are often left in the middle of the chaos, trying to figure out what they're supposed to do.

To best serve student athletes, we need to dispel the myth of the so-called mega deals. A 2024 report by NIL Assist on NCAA.org sheds some light on the reality of NIL opportunities, particularly outside the spotlight of football and basketball. According to the report, the median deal value for a social media post for athletes in sports other than the top revenue-generating ones is just $100 per post. This is a stark contrast to the headlines featuring multi-million-dollar deals.

The reality is that large-scale contracts are outliers, not the norm. Even with the anticipation of revenue sharing as a proposed solution for schools to negotiate and pay their top recruits in the coming years, the average paid player payout will be in the range of tens of thousands of dollars per year, due to a proposed revenue sharing cap. That's nothing to sneeze at, but it's a far cry from the multi-million-dollar NIL headlines that garner the most media attention. Rather than chasing unrealistic expectations, it's far more beneficial for parents and students to focus on creating a personalized roadmap for success in NIL—a roadmap tailored to the individual student athlete's unique circumstances that will help them to maximize their potential without falling prey to the distorted views often pushed by the media.

Athletic departments and coaches are working hard to incorporate NIL strategies into their programs, offering support and education to their athletes. However, it's a numbers game. The vast amount of information included in NIL education can be overwhelming. It sometimes feels like reading dense material from an accounting, finance, or sports law class, but that's because much of the curriculum out there is designed to keep athletes compliant with the rules. However, it falls short when it comes to empowering them to take control of their own NIL journey.

Every student athlete needs a more individualized approach because their NIL value depends on a variety of unique factors, from their personal brand to their sport, interests, and following. University athletic departments are not currently staffed to negotiate personal contracts and marketing deals for every individual athlete. They're also not equipped to build out personalized NIL strategies or find deals for each of the five-hundred-plus student athletes they support each year. The onus is on you and your athlete to create opportunities. However, without a clear, personalized strategy, your athlete may struggle to tap into their full NIL potential.

Unfortunately, the media's focus on exaggerated mega deals often sets unrealistic expectations for student athletes. Many begin to view NIL as a golden ticket, a windfall of easy money that will just be handed to them. When the reality fails to match the fantasy, these same athletes can end up feeling disappointed and frustrated.

Therefore, our goals should be to set realistic expectations for NIL and to equip all student athletes with the tools, leadership, mentorship, and support they need to succeed. It's not about following the crowd or getting caught up in the headline-driven hype. True success in NIL comes from understanding the landscape, developing a clear plan, and being willing to put in the work to create sustainable, long-term opportunities and relationships.

MISCONCEPTIONS ABOUT NIL

A lot of parents and coaches were concerned when the NIL rule change was enacted because they thought NIL would distract student athletes from their academics or athletics. Coaches, in particular, worried that NIL opportunities could lead to a loss of loyalty, with star athletes jumping into the transfer portal, or that NIL might cause a deterioration of team morale. Would NIL foster competition between teammates, weaken team bonding, or create tension in the locker room?

While all of these concerns are understandable, it turns out they are largely unfounded. A recent survey, which included over a thousand student athletes, specifically addressed these issues. The results revealed that NIL opportunities had had an overwhelmingly positive impact on student athletes, with no significant evidence to suggest that NIL causes distractions from academics or athletics. The survey found zero statistical evidence to support the idea that NIL leads to locker room tension or team conflict, with just 6 percent of the athletes reporting any change in perceived jealousy or resentment at all.[5] Instead, student athletes see NIL as an exciting additional avenue to explore that neither shifts their focus nor negatively affects their day-to-day lives.

This is an important myth to dispel, so let me say it again as clearly as I can. **NIL is not undermining the academic or athletic focus of student athletes**; it is simply providing them with new opportunities that they are eager to pursue. There are outliers, of course, but NIL is seen as a net positive by student athletes at large.

In fact, let's look at a few other misconceptions about NIL. Here are a few things that NIL is *not*:

NIL is not pay-for-play. Despite the sensational headlines that make it seem like collectives are just paying athletes to transfer or play, NIL deals come with contractual obligations. Athletes must uphold these obligations to receive payment. NIL is a contract, an agreement that requires the athlete to behave professionally and deliver on the terms outlined—whether that's by promoting a brand, making appearances, or creating content.

NIL is also not a golden ticket that guarantees money just for being an athlete. It requires effort, professionalism, and fulfillment of responsibilities toward numerous partners and stakeholders in each deal. Do collective payments under the guise of NIL happen today? Yes, they do. However, expect the future of collective deals to have more contractual rigor. They will continue to include "true NIL" obligations, responsibilities, and payments subject to the player's NIL usage. Even if schools are allowed to pay players under a proposed revenue-share model in the future, NIL deals will continue to supplement the pool of funding for top recruits, but not without true NIL commitments to appearances, autograph signings, events, licensing, and more.

Finally, **NIL is not limited to football and basketball**, Division I athletes, the top 1 or 2 percent of athletes, or those who are likely to go pro. Since NIL is about ownership of an athlete's name, image, and likeness—and the right to leverage those assets in the marketplace, the opportunity is open to any athlete willing to take ownership of their personal brand.

Navigating the world of NIL opportunities isn't just about scoring high-profile endorsements; it's about cultivating a platform that lasts well beyond college. While many athletes focus on short-term gains, those with a long-game approach understand that NIL is a foundation for building a lasting legacy.

Take Jack Betts, a D3 football player from Amherst College, as an example. Despite not being an NFL Draft prospect, Betts took the initiative to carve out his place in the NIL landscape, securing hundreds of deals and partnerships. His proactive mindset led him to found Make Your Own Legacy Academy, an NIL development company, all while pursuing his master's degree. Betts exemplifies the power of leveraging college athletics to build a personal brand that extends far beyond the field. While no one can predict the future, I'd place a strong "bet on Betts" to succeed in the long game of life, driven by his early leadership and vision in the NIL space.

AVOIDING SHINY OBJECT SYNDROME

NIL represents the greatest opportunity of our generation for student athletes, particularly those with business, brand marketing, or entrepreneurial aspirations, to take control of their futures in ways that were once unimaginable. However, with this unprecedented opportunity also comes the risk of falling for what I call the *shiny object syndrome*. Glittery short-term choices can have long-term opportunity costs.

The NIL landscape is brimming with glittery and enticing prospects, from marketplaces promising exposure to brand partnerships and deals to newly minted NIL agents and professional service providers eager to capitalize on this emerging economy. It's almost like a land grab for student athlete NIL. And if you're not clear on your goals and vision, it's easy to get swept up in the buffet of opportunities without a clear strategy, wasting a lot of time and energy in the process. Student athletes often find themselves grasping at anything that looks promising, but this approach is the opposite of strategic planning. It can lead to burnout, personal brand dilution, conflicts of interest, or worse consequences when decisions are made in haste.

On the darker side of NIL, there's a growing problem of sketchy practices targeting student athletes. Many students are receiving direct messages through social media from aggressive marketers, promoters, and professional service providers. These suitors often promise free merchandise or the chance to be part of a big promotion—all they ask in return is for the athlete's personal information (like their home address). These pitches may sound appealing, especially when they offer what seem like easy perks, but they should raise major red flags for any parent.

Students eager to make quick gains might end up in bad deals, which can lead to frustration, loss of confidence, signing away future NIL rights, or worst-case scenario, compromised safety. Sadly, this is happening more frequently, so it's important to stay focused and informed. Student athletes must have a clear vision of what they want to build long-term, and they must resist the distractions that shiny objects present.

Shiny object syndrome, simply put, occurs when someone shifts their focus to new and trendy ideas, neglecting what they're currently working on or what they've strategically planned. Rushing into deals without first making sure that they align with your goals and vision often leads to expensive detours and setbacks.

Additionally, when student athletes chase every deal that comes their way, they risk chipping away at their NIL value. Without a clear set of standards and an understanding of how to align with a brand and their own unique selling proposition, they can quickly become commoditized.

As parents, coaches, or mentors, we must help our rising leaders develop a clear vision and strong discernment to safeguard their NIL future. By avoiding the allure of short-term distractions and focusing on strategic, value-driven decisions, athletes can grow their NIL value steadily and avoid the pitfalls that come with poorly chosen partnerships.

WHO WILL DO THE HEAVY LIFTING?

Finally, we need to address a common misconception that many parents have about NIL. You see, many parents assume that their child's school will do the heavy lifting when it comes to NIL. This is simply not the case, with the exception of a very few top recruits.

Schools deserve praise for ramping up their support, training, and efforts in recent years to facilitate NIL for their student athletes. However, school administrations are often overwhelmed by competing deadlines, limited funds, the changing legal landscape and constrained resources. They simply do not have the capacity to offer individualized attention to every one of the hundreds of athletes under their care each year.

Even with the best intentions, schools are hamstrung by competing priorities and the rapid pace of change in the NIL space. An administration might have a team of one or even three NIL-focused staff members, but when you consider the hundreds of athletes they're responsible for, the math simply doesn't work. These departments cannot be expected to provide a personalized strategy for every athlete.

So while your child's school will be a valuable partner in their NIL journey, they are not going to be the drivers of ultimate NIL success—nor should they be. Turning over complete control of your NIL strategy to an institution is not the answer. Instead, athletes should see their schools, coaches, and administrators as aligned contributors to their goals—partners who add value to their NIL platform but who are not the architects of their success.

The role of a great coach or a supportive athletic department is to provide wind at a student's back, but at the end of the day, the student still needs to be prepared to fly on their own. True NIL success requires them to own their own opportunities and strategic planning beyond what the school can offer. Ultimately, it is up to each student athlete to build their NIL platform and navigate this space with purpose and intention.

Finally, let me offer some encouragement to parents. NIL represents a powerful leadership development opportunity, not only for student athletes but for their families as well. This is a chance for parents to partner with their students, providing support and guidance while still allowing them to take the lead. Again, it's just like when your child first learned to drive. As a parent, your heart raced a bit faster when you handed over the keys and let them venture out on their own, fully aware of the potholes in the road, the unpredictable drivers, and the many obstacles they would inevitably encounter.

But just as you did then, you have to trust them now. Handing over the keys to their personal NIL journey is an important step in allowing them to grow, learn, and develop the skills to navigate challenges on their own. It's totally normal to feel nervous about the potential hazards, but it's equally important to let them drive their own goals and strategies.

As parents, our role is to support them in their growth, to be there when they need guidance, and to help them steer around the potholes and road hazards that come their way. It can be a little scary, but the goal is to trust them, hope their mistakes are small and manageable, and watch them build something meaningful. Their NIL journey, like driving, is about independence, responsibility, and growth—and we must let them take the wheel while knowing that we're always there when they need us.

CHAPTER SEVEN

PLATFORMULA FOR SUCCESS

WHEN IT COMES to winning with NIL, building a *brand* isn't enough. Contrary to what some brand consultants may say, an athlete is *not* a brand—they are the *owner* of a brand. This personal business brand carries influence across networks, communities, programs, teams, and alma maters. However, an athlete's brand assets (name, image, likeness, and reputation) can't be fully leveraged without a *platform*.

Branding your name, image, and likeness is just the start. A brand can evolve, adapt, and be curated to fit into the owner's strategy and long-term goals. Just remember to separate the brand (e.g., asset/reputation) from the brand owner (the athlete). This perspective will make all the difference in how you manage your strategic decision-making and elevate your full potential. Your brand is your reputation in the marketplace, but it doesn't encompass *all* that you are as an athlete or a human.

How you establish yourself as a platform owner—a business owner leveraging an NIL brand to gain partnerships, visibility, and influence—depends on how you set up your platform. This requires tools, services, and offerings (some of which can be creator content) that serve your stakeholders and partners best.

The foundational work to empower your platform goes beyond branding checklists. It's about being more than an "online version of sports-girl Susie"—it's about being an NIL *platform owner*, a founder, builder, expander, and entrepreneur who establishes a platform with offerings, services, and processes that attract, manage, and maintain super healthy relationships with brand partners, institutions, networks, and other platform-building opportunities that come your way as a result of what you've created with your NIL. Your platform supports and enables this entire ecosystem.

NIL *builders*, *founders*, and *expanders* (i.e., athlete entrepreneurs) must construct a platform to capitalize on NIL opportunities. Building a brand for yourself doesn't go far enough; it must support expansion, growth, leverage, and long-term impact. Your brand doesn't expand your influence—your platform does. A platform enables you to serve others who want to connect with what you have to offer. Your brand defines who aligns with your mission and whom you're called to serve. It's the "tuning fork" that shapes your services, audience, and ideal partners. However, the expansion, growth, leverage, and earning potential come from a platform that maximizes your NIL assets to increase your reach, influence, income, and impact.

If you have a brand but no platform, then you have an asset that will grow at a snail's pace or even be left behind without the platform tools and systems to accelerate reach, influence, and income. You risk wasting your greatness and potential on unleveraged, one-off projects and distractions, which may result in being left behind in an accelerating landscape. Not to mention the risk of having your identity wrapped up in your "brand" alone.

If you have a platform but no brand, you're leaving value on the table by not clearly defining whom you serve and what they can expect from you as defined by your brand and reputation. Your brand reputation needs to stand out with a distinct position that carves a unique space and value in the marketplace. Marketability is key. Most high school and college-aged athletes have a large supportive ecosystem at their fingertips, but it requires a vision and understanding of how to position your brand.

To increase income, influence, and impact, you need both a brand and a platform. And this isn't something you can define once, set, and forget. It's an ownership commitment to maintain, revisit, communicate your vision, expand, grow, innovate, and continuously improve long after your collegiate "game" ends.

Why is becoming a platform owner so critical? As a professional platform owner myself, here's what I know it takes to build an expansive, robust NIL presence and platform: It takes ownership perspective and skills—both adaptive and technical—to operate as a center of excellence and rise to the top of the game. These skills aren't gained from deploying one-off managers, subject matter advisors, or institutional counselors with limited time and resources to make all the decisions on your behalf. They're part of your ecosystem, but *you* are the backbone and owner of your platform. As the owner, you put the pieces in place to create value and vision. I'm going to teach you how to own your NIL and your future earning potential.

Why now? There has never been a time like this. NIL presents a *huge* opportunity in a shifting landscape. I'm so passionate about this that I left the tech industry in order to help college athletes and their parents realize the massive potential at their fingertips. You are quite literally at the *tip of the sword* for what will become NIL platforms, founders, business owners, and entrepreneurs shaping our future in the coming decades.

For decades, college athletes have taken their leadership skills into the "real world" and achieved long-term success. The difference now is that athletes and their families can accelerate the development of these critical skills, gain a headstart on building momentum for their platforms, and ensure they remain "ahead of the game" in life after sports. I'm committed to helping student athletes and their families turn today's chaos into tomorrow's competitive advantage. The best way to do that is by building a sustainable platform to support your success.

Your value as a person is infinite. Don't confuse your NIL "valuation" with your worth as a human being. There is a vast future ahead, so seize the momentum and never sell yourself short.

THE PLATFORM OWNER'S POWER FORMULA

Building your platform is like constructing a bridge to future success. The stronger and more flexible it is, the more it can support growth and withstand the winds of change. Just like the Golden Gate Bridge in San Francisco, a platform built on a firm foundation but with the flexibility to adapt will endure and thrive.

There's no set "playbook" for this new NIL era. The winners now are creatively shaping a future where they write their own rules. While I can't predict the future, I do have a proven framework for building a platform that can bend, flex, and adapt to support your personal growth, strategy, collaboration, and opportunities. This framework—a clear, value-building directive—is the PLATFORMULA.

You don't have to take my word for it; you can experience the formula yourself. This platform-building process is meant to be personalized and adaptable to your goals. The PLATFORMULA process allows you to proactively flex, adapt, and accelerate your competitive advantages while preparing to seize opportunities with an ownership mindset.

Building a platform requires both a formula and a series of actionable steps:

First, let's take a look at the formula, which is key for platform owners to internalize and understand. The Platform Owner's Power Formula identifies where your growth levers are to unlock hidden potential and lead in this new landscape. In order to own your full potential and see your platform gaining powerful momentum, you'll need to orchestrate an ecosystem based on these principles:

The Platform Owner's Power (POP) Formula:
(Perspective + Shared Vision) x (Collaboration) x (Clear Priorities) = Leveraged, Adaptable, Accelerating Platform Growth.

Before diving into the phases of building your platform, let's examine why this formula is essential for any platform owner as an assessment to boost your potential.

Perspective + Shared Vision: The greater your perspective and shared vision, the more your platform can expand. Perspective is your ability to make sense of situations, understand them, and lead effectively. It's a continuously growing asset. Even the most senior CEOs and leading brand marketers understand the need to expand their perspective to achieve better outcomes. This perspective drives a shared vision, which grows as more people understand and invest in it. As a platform owner, developing these leadership areas will be vital in navigating this new landscape. Your platform's power and potential will only be limited by your ability to expand your perspective and shared vision as the owner and visionary leader.

Force Multipliers—Collaboration and Clear Priorities: The growth of your platform's "flywheel effect" depends on two factors under your ownership:

Collaboration: The more aligned and open to collaboration you are, the more valuable your platform becomes. Your primary role is to elevate others. By using your talents to create win-win scenarios, you make your platform a space that is conducive to contributions, which expands your platform's value and impact. Do you see how the effect of elevating others to create value for them and help them achieve their goals becomes a force that elevates your value as well?

Clear Priorities: The only way to accelerate a complex ecosystem of collaborations is by having streamlined, focused priorities. You can't chase every opportunity; instead, you must deliberately align your platform's vision and growth with your most effective partnerships and actions. Your priorities are your values, principles, and strategy in action. Without these pillars, the platform can falter. Focused priorities help you avoid distractions, enabling you to "win" rather than "spin." You exponentially expand your platform's value by staying clear and focused on priorities aligned with your shared vision.

On a regular basis, especially as you're getting started, it's important to revisit each piece of the formula and assess where you, as the platform owner, can initiate further momentum and clarity.

PLATFORMULA FOR SUCCESS

By following the Platformula and its principles, you'll create a robust and adaptable foundation for success that aligns with both your personal goals and long-term impact.

Now that you understand the key principles for realizing your platform potential, let's look at what it takes to *really* invest in your platform for future success, and the Platformula process that can get you from where you are now to the bright future ahead.

This process can be visualized as a flywheel—building a platform is like setting up a merry-go-round that generates its own momentum. Over time, each turn of the wheel builds on the momentum of the previous one, allowing your platform to gain speed and impact with less effort, even as you onboard more collaborators and stakeholders.

To make this possible, you must be willing to "get out of your own way." Detach from your NIL, and start viewing it as an investor views an asset, deciding where to invest more if the return looks promising. The Platform Owner's Power Formula identifies the key areas of investment and growth. As a parent, you're an investor in your child, and your child must be the primary investor in building their NIL platform.

Initially, it may feel a little callous or emotionally distant to adopt this investor perspective, but it's a critical long-term view. This approach prevents tying worth or value solely to athletic success. As the saying goes, "see the forest through the trees." If you're too close to the project or overly tied to your identity within the NIL space, you risk missteps because you can't see the big picture. Viewing NIL as an asset and your family as the investors allows you to make decisions that support growth and avoid actions that could limit potential.

Every small commitment made now reduces room for other priorities later. Time, talent, and resources invested in "short-term shiny things" come with the opportunity cost of potentially more strategic moves just around the corner.

To make the most of these changes and opportunities, you must adopt a *platform ownership perspective* for the future. But what exactly is this "platform ownership perspective"? It's a mindset shift from merely managing NIL deals to strategically building a sustainable platform that maximizes future potential, aligns with long-term goals, and creates lasting impact.

OWNERSHIP: WHY (AND WHY NOT) TO BUILD A PLATFORM

Before we dive into *why* you should build a platform, let's first consider *why you shouldn't*:

- **Building a Platform Requires Investment.** Establishing a valuable platform takes time, talent, and energy. There's no shortcut or overnight success in this endeavor. You need to be ready to learn, take action, and seek real feedback to grow your platform. This journey requires commitment to a long-term path of evolution and growth—one that may look very different from others. If you're not interested in long-term growth and prosperity, or if you're just looking for a quick way to cash in on NIL or other short-term goals, platform building may not be the best use of your time and energy.

- **Consistency and Showing Up Matter.** If you struggle to finish what you start or want a "set-it-and-forget-it" solution, platform building may not be for you. Success requires steady engagement, reliability, and enthusiasm to show up for others. Building a platform means consistently committing your time and professionalism to grow a trustworthy presence.

- **Platform Building Brings Visibility and Responsibility.** As your platform grows, so do your responsibilities and decisions. With greater visibility, you'll face more complex partnerships, growth opportunities, and exposure. *With great power comes great responsibility*, as Spider-man once said. And with increased "surface area" comes increased responsibility. Building a platform requires intentional decision-making and careful consideration of the entire ecosystem you're creating. If you're more comfortable as a "one-person show," consider whether you want to build a platform whose purpose is to serve others at an ever-growing capacity.

By understanding why you *shouldn't* build a platform, you can make an informed choice about whether platform building is the right path for you and your athlete's NIL endeavors.

Now, let's examine the benefits a platform can offer:

- **Leverage:** Your platform allows you to use assets like your name, image, and likeness across various contexts, maximizing their value and impact. It allows you to use your gifts and maximize your influence and impact. This is what leverage looks like in action.

- **Velocity:** Having a platform in place accelerates your "time to market" and empowers you to make faster, stronger decisions in partnerships, collaborations, and business deals. With established systems, you can take advantage of new opportunities without having to build from scratch each time.

- **New Value Creation:** Building a platform enables *combinatorial innovation*, the ability to create new value by joining forces with your ecosystem of partners and collaborators. Take Hello Kitty, for example. The brand has remained valuable for decades, with its parent company, Sanrio, continually increasing its worth by collaborating with other major players. Hello Kitty x Nike? Check. Hello Kitty x Pixi Cosmetics? Yes. Hello Kitty x Sugarfina candy? Absolutely. Sanrio combines assets to innovate and create new market value, benefiting companies, stakeholders, and audiences alike.

If you're considering building a platform for long-term success, ask yourself this key question: *Will the capabilities I want to develop serve multiple partners, use cases, and future scenarios?* Are you building capabilities to serve just one purpose—like NIL cash today—or to support multiple purposes, partnerships, and future use cases after your days in sports are over?

If your answer is yes to multiple future use cases, then let's get started building your powerful platform.

PRINCIPLES AND PILLARS FOR BUILDING A GREAT PLATFORM

- **Trust Above Everything**—To be trustworthy, you need consistency over time. Whether in NIL activities, business, or future endeavors, your success is built on the capabilities of your platform. As the platform owner, it's essential to prioritize trust, ensuring your platform is reliable, predictable, and secure for others. Consistency, integrity, and professionalism foster reliability, making partners feel secure in engaging with you.

- **Long-Term Perspective: Vision, Mission, Strategy—** Identify and align with your core values before taking on partners and collaborators; otherwise, it will be difficult to determine what aligns with your goals. Ask yourself: What do you stand for? Remember: *what you stand for* represents your platform's mission and vision, while *what makes you stand out* is your branding. Branding is an asset, but it's distinct from the long-term vision and mission that will drive your platform.

- **Strategic Decision-Making—**Platform owners make thoughtful, measured choices. As the saying goes, "measure twice, cut once." Strategic decision-making means prioritizing and designing your platform with the big picture in mind rather than making decisions purely for short-term gains. We'll delve deeper into long-term versus short-term thinking in the coming chapters.

- **Ecosystem Enablement—**Your platform enables a thriving ecosystem with win-win-win scenarios. Platform owners understand that their platform benefits everyone within it, creating exponential value as more people engage. This approach fosters a network where you win, your partners win, and the broader ecosystem wins as well.

In my PLATFORMULA process and programs, we focus on developing these essential platform capabilities so that you can enable and support the valuable ecosystem around you. The capabilities you build are portable—your platform isn't tied to one school, social media outlet, collective, company, employer, or brand partner. It's *your* platform to carry into all future endeavors, creating a foundation for long-term success.

WHY WE DO IT

The PLATFORMULA Process is a method for amplifying growth and opportunities unlike any other for sports families to grow together. To be successful in this new landscape and build a powerful platform that will propel you forward toward a bright future, it takes ownership and action. Growth happens in action and in relationships—and both are requirements in our interactive PLATFORMULA process. I provide the guidance, steps and framework to help you build your platform, along with an ecosystem of support to secure your first NIL deals, form and manage your brand and business, and drive momentum. This is the approach we take at NIL Builders Group.

At the core of our work is empowering student athletes and their families with the capabilities to achieve long-term success, impact, and income, even amid an unpredictable landscape. The NIL space provides real-time opportunities to gain valuable experience, but it's seeing your family's long-game legacy take shape that drives our passion. Our process and programs are designed for those aiming to create a lasting legacy. All of our programs incorporate these three pillars for the success of your sports family:

- **Build:** We focus on building the athlete's personal brand, business acumen, and platform owner potential

by providing the foundational structures necessary for success. We partner with parents to bridge their involvement and evolution of their own powerful platform to support their athlete.
- **Belong:** Programs that involve group coaching, family participation, and in-person events emphasize the importance of community, collaboration, and networking, allowing participants to belong to a supportive network of peers, mentors, and partners.
- **Become:** Leadership development is a key component, with programs designed to help participants become adaptable, forward-thinking leaders who can navigate and thrive in the volatile, uncertain, complex, and ambiguous (VUCA) landscape of modern athletics and in life beyond sports.

By ensuring each program aligns with these pillars, participants are guided through a comprehensive journey that not only develops their skills and platforms but also integrates them into a community and transforms them into leaders equipped for future challenges.

We believe that lifting others is essential to rising to your own potential. To step into greatness and reach full potential, one must serve others with their gifts. Your platform enables you to do this, collaborating with others while propelling you toward your biggest goals. Beyond guiding you in platform building, we focus on developing your inner agility and modern leadership skills so you can both own your futures—as a parent and as an athlete.

THE PLATFORMULA PROCESS

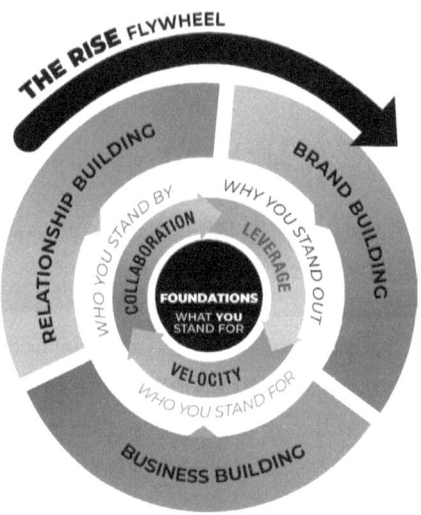

STAGE 1—FOUNDATIONS

A platform is only as reliable as its foundation. It's what you stand on, what elevates you, and what you stand for as you build a platform to uplift others. Our first stage centers on identifying your platform pillars: the core values, principles, and beliefs—whether you're the athlete or a parent supporting one. Here, we clarify your big vision, mission, and unique gifts meant to serve others and create value for years to come. This stage provides clarity and direction for the rest of your platform-building efforts.

STAGE 2—BRAND BUILDING

This stage involves packaging and positioning your values to help you stand out. You'll develop your brand identity, understand your audience, define your offerings, and carve out a unique position to maximize marketability.

STAGE 3—BUSINESS BUILDING—FORMATION AND ENTREPRENEURIAL ACTIVITIES

We cover the practical aspects of business: contracts, legalities, taxes, and financial management to ensure you're creating and protecting assets and value effectively. We explore the ownership mindset in action and take the first steps toward understanding sales, marketing, and partnerships in the context of your NIL activities and platform building. This is where your unique point of view, talents, and vision start to take shape, and your personalized strategy comes together.

STAGE 4—RELATIONSHIP BUILDING—COLLABORATION ENABLEMENT

In this stage, you scale your platform with systems, support, collaborations, and ongoing improvements to expand and sustain growth. We provide a space to build those relationship skills, surround yourself with elite subject matter experts, and gain access to early partnership momentum to power up your growth. First, it's fine-tuning your collaboration and relationship enablement. Then you can harness the network effect that kicks into gear.

STAGE 5—THE RISE

If you're familiar with the flywheel effect, that's precisely what we're initiating at NIL Builders Group. The *PLATFORMULA* process is designed to create a system that builds leverage, speed, and scalable value. Each "spin" of the wheel builds momentum, making the process increasingly self-propelling. The result is a growth trajectory for your platform that continuously amplifies your impact, influence, and income.

This stage is where your foundational work begins to pay off, and momentum becomes a force of its own to continue to propel your entire platform growth. You'll maximize your feedback "reps," see faster iterative improvements, and begin to show up bigger as a result of having these sources of inspiration continually working for you and your athlete. This stage requires five inputs to see the exponential growth rate outputs. I call them the **Flywheel Five:**

1. Peers
2. Parents
3. Brand Partners
4. Business Mentors
5. Athletic Mentors (Coaches, Trainers, Administrative support, etc).

Not only do we teach the fundamentals to establish this flywheel as your platform, but we also equip you, as the platform owner, to handle mindset shifts, manage the mental load, and navigate the increasing complexity that comes with leadership. Brands, companies, and potential partners want to work with athletes who show up as leaders, build trust, and maintain professionalism in any endeavor from start to finish.

Leveling up your leadership as a role within your thriving platform and systems is key. Platform building is a process, but the experience of taking action is one of the greatest leadership development opportunities available to student athletes today.

CAPACITY AND LEADERSHIP DEVELOPMENT

Throughout each phase, we facilitate your growth in two key ways—through action and through relationships. It's important to invest in building your own assets, but when you do so alongside like-minded peers, supporters, partners, experts, and mentors, your growth can accelerate significantly in a short period. These relationships provide a space for deep conversations and meaningful connections, amplifying your development.

For your potential to flourish, you must be planted in the right environments. This is crucial. Even if you choose not to work with our team or follow our process, it's essential to surround yourself with relationships that will strengthen and help you grow. Often, this means putting yourself in spaces where you're consistently challenged to step out of your comfort zone. Growth isn't about having people who only "cheer you on" and praise every move; it's about engaging with those who push you to discover what you're truly capable of in action.

You need an environment where you can stretch, learn, and develop your unique talents and gifts beyond sports. To reach your potential, you must play full out and lean into growth at your personal edges.

Every college athlete has the power to turn their platform into a self-propelling asset. This journey involves two key components: mastering the Platform Power formula, where you own and elevate your unique strengths, and progressing through each stage of PLATFORMULA development to solidify your brand for long-term success.

Unlock Your Platform Potential

Ready to take the first step? Learn more about our work at NIL Builders Group and discover how we can guide you through this transformative process. Schedule a free strategy call with our team today to start your path toward a resilient, impactful platform. Book your call today at www.nilbuildersgroup.com

CHAPTER EIGHT
SHORT-TERM GAINS VERSUS LONG-TERM SUCCESS

YOU CAN SUCCEED today while building up tomorrow, but it takes intentional strategy and decision-making. So how can you master a long-term perspective and strategic decision-making so you avoid shiny objects? Well, there are two key indicators that can help you determine whether you're approaching NIL opportunities with a short-term perspective or a long-term mindset.

The first of these indicators is a false sense of urgency. Short-term thinking often comes with a sense of urgency that's not real but manufactured. This urgency can be driven by fear of missing out (FOMO)—the feeling that if everyone else is at the party, you need to be there too. If a lot of other athletes are signing the latest video game deal, you may feel compelled to jump on board, even if it's not aligned with your values or goals.

Beware of the inner voice that whispers things like, *This is a once-in-a-lifetime opportunity*, or, *If I don't take this deal, the money will go to someone else, and I'll miss out*. Another red flag is the temptation to do a misaligned campaign "just this one time," with the intention of adjusting course later. These thoughts are common when you're focused on fitting in rather than standing out.

The allure of short-term gains can be powerful, and it can be difficult to resist the temptation of a quick payday or the appeal of doing what everyone else is doing. But as parents and partners in our student athletes' journeys, our role is to be a sounding board. We need to help them recognize the red flags that come with false urgency and short-term thinking to talk through whether a deal is truly a smart move or just a distraction from their long-term goals.

Shiny objects and distractions tend to revolve around money—those quick, flashy deals that seem too good to pass up. I've seen parents get caught in this short-term thinking trap, too. Your athlete's value will continue to rise as they mature and develop. Long-term thinking recognizes that the true value of your athlete's NIL goes far beyond the immediate monetary benefits. It's about the forty-year perspective, not just the four-year flash in the pan. The long-term view appreciates the non-monetary benefits that far outweigh short-term financial gains.

STANDING OUT VERSUS FITTING IN

Early on in sports, athletes are often encouraged to be utility players: versatile and able to fit into any role. As they get older, they become more specialized, but most young athletes can relate to being a utility player during their early years, able to fit into any role on the team. And while that flexibility can be valuable on the field, in the NIL space, it's important to avoid becoming merely a commodity. You don't want to be someone who just dives into every opportunity that comes your way.

SHORT-TERM GAINS VERSUS LONG-TERM SUCCESS

Instead, you want to stand out by having a unique perspective and a clear, long-term vision.

This is where the power of long-term thinking comes into play. Don't grab every deal just because it's there. Instead, carefully curate your opportunities so they align with your personal brand, your values, and your long-term goals. Success is sustained through strategy. Ultimately, the goal is to build something lasting, something that distinguishes you from the rest—not just in the next four years, but for the next forty.

Yes, the temptation to take the easy route is strong. It's easy to say yes to every opportunity that comes along, but knowing when to say no is what truly sets you on the right path.

Let me share a personal story. When I was growing my business, several of my entrepreneurial mentors and peers suggested I jump on TikTok. At the time, TikTok was starting to pick up steam, and given my background in dance and cheerleading, they believed I could easily create content, attract followers, and grow my presence on that platform. Since my goal was to grow my brand, their advice seemed sound.

And, honestly, they weren't wrong *in theory*. I love dance videos. I've probably watched more hours of choreography videos than most tween girls. So it wasn't that I didn't like TikTok or dance videos—I loved them. But I wasn't just looking for growth in numbers. I needed to attract the *right* audience, the people who were aligned with my message and mission.

While TikTok might have been an easy platform for me to create and post content, I decided to say no. Even now, I'm not on TikTok, and there's a good reason for that. I knew it would be a distraction from my podcast and the other platforms where I am truly adding value and attracting the right kind of followers. Although some of my peers have grown enormous TikTok followings, and I genuinely applaud their efforts and success, I can confidently say it wasn't for me. Fortunately, I had the discernment to recognize that, for my goals, it wasn't the right fit.

Give yourself permission to say no, even when an opportunity seems good on the surface. It's not always a black-or-white decision. You're not always choosing between something obviously good or bad. Some opportunities exist in a gray area, so you need to understand how even a small commitment—like signing up to be a TikTok creator—might slow you down from reaching your larger goals.

When you're faced with opportunities, ask yourself if they align with your long-term vision. Will this decision propel you toward your goals, or will it become a detour that slows down your progress? It's important to develop that sense of discernment, to have what I call a "short-term decision-making tuning fork," so you can make choices that keep you on the path toward your ultimate success instead of getting caught up in every shiny object that comes your way.

TikTok might be the right choice for other people, but it was the wrong choice for me. It's important to recognize that just because something works for someone else doesn't mean you have to jump on the bandwagon. You don't have to chase an opportunity just because it's popular. What matters is whether it aligns with your goals and your vision.

KEY QUESTIONS FOR LONG-TERM THINKING

Long-term thinking starts with two key questions: **Where are you going? And where are you growing?**

These are two things I like to explore when I'm helping someone clarify their vision of success or long-term goals.

"Where are you going?" can take many forms. It could be a specific outcome, a material result, or even a personal development improvement. There's likely more than one answer to this question, but they all converge into a coherent vision that guides you forward.

"Where are you growing?" is just as important. This is about recognizing areas where you have opportunities to strengthen yourself, as well as where the pitfalls could sneak up on you. Remember: Long-term thinking is about making decisions based on where you're going and being willing to make uncomfortable short-term choices to accelerate your momentum in the long run. Sometimes, the harder decision in the short term sets the stage for greater ease and momentum in the future.

Long-term thinking is ultimately rooted in clarity, knowing where you're going, understanding where you need to grow, and then applying that perspective to your day-to-day decision-making.

THE REAL VALUE OF YOUR STUDENT'S NIL

So how can you determine the real long-term value of your student athlete's NIL? First, there's the technical value of their NIL as an asset. But then there's the deeper, more significant value that comes from what the athlete learns in the process of pursuing NIL opportunities and owning their platform. That learning is the real prize.

Several factors contribute to an athlete's NIL value, and it all circles back to knowing where you're going, where you're growing, who you serve, and how you can serve them to the best of your ability. It's about putting your unique gifts to work for others, not just capitalizing on your athletic skills.

What matters most is how clear your vision is and how grounded you are in your core values, and NIL value isn't limited to sports. You don't want to be just another athlete; you also need to show people who you are beyond your sport, what you aspire to be, who your audience is, and what you want them to gain from being connected to you. Your NIL value is about serving others with your true gifts, not just your athletic prowess.

The most common mistake I see with athletes undermining their NIL value is that they try to build their NIL value backward, from the top down. They prioritize vanity metrics, like their follower count on social media, or player stats and performance. They engage in short-term, scarcity thinking and attempt to grasp onto any NIL deals that come across their desk without discernment. And then they wonder why they're not standing out, getting better deals, or making money. That's all short-term, incremental stuff. You have to build your real NIL value from the foundation up. The influence, impact, and income will follow.

It all starts with a clear sense of self, vision, and purpose. That's how you build real, sustainable value in the NIL space. With a solid foundation, you can then begin to add incremental value by diving deeper into factors like the demographics of your sport, the size of your market, your on-field performance, and your current or desired social media following. You can also consider the level of support you may or may not receive from your institution to bolster your personalized strategy.

Remember: The value of NIL extends far beyond monetary benefits. NIL provides the chance to build real-world partnerships, enhance your communication and leadership skills, and make meaningful connections—all while engaging in activities that are fun and unique to your position as a student athlete.

SHORT-TERM GAINS VERSUS LONG-TERM SUCCESS

When done well, you get to make short-term gains while also building your foundation for long-term success.

I like to think of it as being a "short-term scientist" with a "long-term vision." The first and most important step is always developing that long-term vision. Once that's clear, you can approach short-term strategies with an experimental mindset. In the short term, that means putting on your scientist hat and embracing the idea of experimentation, curiosity, and learning that aligns with your vision.

Also, bear in mind that your first NIL deal doesn't mean you're locked into that brand or partnership forever. Early opportunities can serve as mutually beneficial learning experiences. Once your contractual obligations are fulfilled, you're free to move on, take what you've learned, and improve your next collaboration or partnership. That's what I mean by aligned experimentation.

Short-term gains and long-term success aren't mutually exclusive. You can achieve both in this process, but you do need an intentional strategy and mindset as you go. Just stay grounded in the strong boundaries set by your vision and values. By doing this, you can have fun with the process while ensuring that every step you take contributes to your long-term success.

CHAPTER NINE

DON'T LEAVE POTENTIAL ON THE TABLE

PARENTS AND STUDENT athletes often shortchange themselves by tying their self-worth to external expectations, performance, scorecards, or the opinions of others. We frequently see this in the way individuals, both adults and young people, allow their sense of worth to be dictated by others. For example, in the corporate world, annual performance reviews can become a measure of our self-worth. These reviews are meant to assess how well we meet personal or corporate goals, but they often end up being more than just feedback, affecting our self-worth if we're not careful. Evaluations can become external measuring sticks (or someone else's lens) that we take to heart to define or determine our value. That, in turn, causes us to equate our professional worth with our intrinsic value as human beings.

After more than a decade-and-a-half in the tech industry, I've observed how easy it is for us to get caught up in this cycle. A promotion, a new role, or a nod of approval from senior leadership can make someone feel valuable, while a single bad review can trigger a downward spiral of self-doubt and stress that lingers for months. This corporate scorekeeping isn't unlike what our kids experience in competitive sports, where being benched or not making the cut can feel like a judgment on their very worth.

In the world of sports and recruiting, young athletes are constantly evaluated. Whether they make first string, are relegated to backup, or receive feedback from a coach or a Division I college, they often internalize these external judgments, which can make them believe that their worth is only as high as someone else's rating.

Beyond sports, we see this phenomenon playing out on social media as well. People of all ages, but especially teens and young adults, are bombarded with images and messages that can make them question their worth. Likes, follows, and comments can seem like the ultimate validation or the harshest rejection. This comparison culture has contributed to an epidemic of self-worth issues, particularly in young people, where their mental health suffers as they constantly measure themselves against an often unattainable standard.

We must teach our children (and remind ourselves) that no one—not a boss, not a coach, not social media, and not even family—can dictate your inherent worth. And we must allow positive influences to pour into us whenever possible because the world is full of messages that try to define our value for us. As parents, we have the power to counteract these messages by affirming our child's worth and reminding them that mistakes and setbacks do not diminish their value.

PARENTS SEE THEIR POTENTIAL BEST

Tying our worth to external performance is one of the ways we leave our potential untapped. But if we redefine where we derive our sense of value, we can unlock new levels of growth and fulfillment, both for ourselves and for our children.

No one is better suited for recognizing the true potential of a student athlete than their parents. It might seem obvious, but it's a truth worth repeating: No one knows your child's natural gifts and talents more intimately than you do. While it's always validating to hear a coach praise their athletic skills or a teacher admire their creative genius, these external validations, though valuable, only scratch the surface.

Even the most skilled coaches, mentors, and trainers, who are trained to identify raw talent and coachability, are limited in their ability to see the full picture. They can measure things like sprint time, evaluate the speed of a fastball, or count the number of digs in a volleyball match. But these metrics only capture a small part of what makes your child special.

Beyond the statistics and the scores, there are inherent, God-given gifts and talents that contribute to their success on the field and in life. These are the gifts that have been evident to you since they were young, the unique areas of genius, the natural curiosity and abilities that you, as a parent, have witnessed and nurtured over the years.

This is why it's so important for parents to speak words of encouragement that go beyond game-day preparation. As your child grows older, actively seek opportunities to connect with them on a deeper level. It's easy to get caught up in conversations about homework, schedules, and to-do lists, but your child needs to hear that you see them for who they truly are. They need to know that their worth isn't tied to the number on their jersey but stems from the fact that they are a precious gift.

And if I can get a bit religious, let me add your child was sent here **on** purpose and **for** a purpose. Recognizing their potential means seeing the whole picture, not just their marketability in sports.

Parents also play a central role in helping their student athletes build resilience. As much as we might want to protect our children from taking detours or experiencing setbacks, we cannot—and should not—shield them from these inevitable challenges. Even the most well-behaved kids are going to stumble, fall into ruts, and need to navigate their own paths. These real-life experiences are what build resilience and help them gain the wisdom that only comes from lived experience.

It's not easy for me to say, and it's harder for me to follow it, but the fact is **we must allow our children to fail**. They need to be tested. They need to take off the training wheels and lead themselves, even if it means encountering potholes along the way.

Even so, as parents, we can provide safeguards and support systems that minimize the fallout or damage from their stumbles. To do that, we must maintain a deep connection with our children so we can offer guidance on healthy relationships and equip them with the mindset and tools they'll need when they face inevitable challenges. Most importantly, we must do what we can to instill in them a set of beliefs and a firm foundation of values and principles that will remain constant, no matter where life takes them or how many setbacks they experience.

By framing setbacks as opportunities rather than obstacles, we can help our children develop a leadership mentality, a resilient mindset that empowers them to overcome challenges and get out of ruts. Ultimately, it's about nurturing their potential and helping them grow into the strong, resilient individuals they were meant to be.

As a friend of mine likes to say, the difference between a rut and a grave is how long you stay there. It's a simple yet powerful truth. We all hit potholes. We all go through slumps and face hardships that no one saw coming. But what matters is how you pull yourself back up and how long you allow yourself to stay in that rut before getting back on track. The tools you have in your toolkit—resilience, support systems, and a strong mindset—are what will help you climb out of that rut. And this is where we, as parents, can play an important role by equipping our children to change the flat tire, pull themselves out of the mud, and get back on the road.

POTHOLES TO WATCH OUT FOR

Now, let's talk about some of the specific potholes that student athletes might encounter that could prevent them from reaching their full potential. There are quite a few, and they can be divided into **general student challenges** and those **specific to student athletes**.

One of the most significant potholes is **comparison**. As the saying goes, comparison is the thief of joy, but it's also a major obstacle to realizing your full potential. When a student athlete is constantly comparing themselves to others, they're not in a growth mindset. This is why it's so important to shift them out of comparison mode and into a growth-oriented mindset.

Social media complicates this issue even further. It's always on, and for an inherently competitive person, there's a natural tendency to compare technical skills and achievements with others. This bombardment of comparison can be overwhelming, which makes it all the more important to build a strong foundation of self-worth and values for our student athletes.

Another common pothole is the challenge of **time management**, which is especially difficult for new student athletes. The demands on their time can lead to a lack of sleep, poor diet choices, and overall neglect of their health and well-being—all of which can severely impact their ability to perform at their best.

Additionally, **short-term distractions** or a lack of long-term perspective can hinder their progress. These distractions can misalign their priorities and take their focus away from their long-term goals.

Naivety can also be a problem, especially when entering into binding contracts at this young age. This is new territory. Your athlete needs to build up their discernment in decision-making before signing on the dotted line in any contractual agreement. It's important for them to be in touch with their intuition, not dazzled by glittery salesmanship, and put in their due diligence to learn more about the partners they're entering into agreements with. When money is at stake, it's important to make commitments in a thoughtful, methodical manner, seeking legal guidance when potentially entering into financial and business agreements. Be ready to steady your athlete (and yourself) for encounters that feel "off." Social engineering, empty promises, and predatory behavior are real in this burgeoning NIL landscape. So having a supportive environment and an open line of communication with you, their parent partner, about potential contracts is key to making wise choices.

Another significant challenge is the **limiting beliefs** and stories our children tell themselves about their limitations and self-worth. This is why it's so important to decouple self-worth from performance. If student athletes don't do this, they can find themselves stuck in a slump, feeling limited by their performance or by what's directly in front of them. Without a longer-term perspective, they may start to believe that they are defined by others' opinions or their current situation rather than recognizing that this, too, shall pass and that they are far more than what others say they are.

Finally, we have to acknowledge a common tendency among young people—the tendency to **catastrophize**. I'm not an expert in neuroscience, but it's evident that developing teenage brains and young adults often have a habit of seeing every setback or disappointment as catastrophic. They tend to view decisions, results, and performance as having a permanence that feels overwhelming. In their minds, a setback or a failure can seem like the end of the world.

This mindset is, in part, due to their deep investment in the present moment, but a focus on the here and now can veer into unhealthy territory, where they lose sight of the bigger picture. For many young people, the immediate result or outcome feels like it has the weight of the world behind it. They lack the resilience and life experience—the reps, if you will—to understand that today's challenges are just one part of a much larger story.

Without a long-term perspective, they may not yet grasp that what feels like a devastating failure now could eventually be seen as a valuable lesson. Parents need to help them stay true to their values and remain in action, even when things don't go their way.

Feelings of rejection, peer pressure, and unexpected curveballs are all normal parts of the teenage experience, but they can feel catastrophic in the moment. A perfect example of this played out in the Little League World Series recently. I remember one batter in particular had tears streaming down his face as he stepped up to the plate. There were two outs, runners in scoring positions, and his team was down by one run to keep the World Series championship hopes alive. He had two strikes and tear-streaked cheeks as he stepped back into the batter's box for the pivotal next pitch. He was fully aware of how big the moment was. And yet, despite the pressure, that kid managed to get a hit, which was nothing short of amazing. It's a moment most adults would struggle to handle, but it also highlights just how in tune young people are with their emotions.

As parents, we must recognize and appreciate this emotional intensity while also guiding them through it. Our role is to help them see the bigger picture and understand that not every setback is a catastrophe and the world isn't ending because of one missed opportunity or mistake.

Now, to be clear, these moments of perceived failure are not the biggest risk for student athletes. The biggest risk—the biggest potential pothole—is the pressure to fit in and conform to someone else's expectations or scorecard rather than embracing their unique talents and standing out.

The single greatest obstacle to your child reaching their full potential is if they spend their time trying to fit in instead of recognizing that they were made to stand out. This struggle between fitting in and standing out is where many of the real day-to-day derailments happen. The pressure to conform can be overwhelming, and without the right tools or support, a student athlete may lose sight of their own uniqueness and the gifts they bring to the world.

As parents, it's our job to continually remind them that they were made with unique talents and that they are not meant to blend in but to shine brightly in their own way. It's a tough lesson to teach and even tougher for our teenage kids to fully grasp without experiencing it firsthand, but it's a message they need to hear *often*.

Just remember: It's not our role as parents to fix every problem or smooth out every rough patch for our children. Instead, we should focus on helping them *grow* through their challenges, not just *go* through them.

PLANTING SEEDS FOR THE FUTURE

Building a platform, particularly through NIL, gives your student athlete an exciting opportunity to not only avoid a loss of identity but also gain a stronger sense of self. As we said earlier, NIL is a powerful tool for personal and professional development, and these opportunities offer athletes a chance to develop a "gain of identity," which is essential for their growth beyond the playing field.

Losing your identity is all too common in the world of sports. We hear about it at every level, from professional athletes to college, high school, and even amateur players. The reality is every athlete will eventually face retirement from their sport, whether they want to or not. It's an inevitable part of life.

That loss of identity is most pronounced among professional athletes who have devoted their lives to their sport, but it happens to any athlete who gets deeply involved in their sport. They pour so much time, effort, and passion into it that their entire identity becomes wrapped up in that one pursuit. Then, when the time comes to hang up their uniform—whether due to aging out, injury, or simply not making the cut—it can feel like a part of them is lost forever.

I know because I've been there. I *thought* I was ready to retire from my professional NFL career. Mentally, I was ready. Yet emotionally, the transition still hit me like a ton of bricks. I had to pause and reflect, appreciate, and recalibrate the seeds of potential to water in my next act. But it wasn't easy to take a final bow and depart from an identity that I had known for decades.

Those who cultivate a "gain of identity" beyond their sport are the ones who are most likely to transition successfully into the next chapter of their lives because they've planted seeds of potential that can blossom after their sports career ends. On the other hand, those who fail to build an identity outside of sports often find themselves spinning in circles, struggling to figure out who they are outside of their sport.

What does NIL have to do with this search for identity? NIL provides a fertile ground where the seeds of potential can be planted, and athletes can water those seeds, whether or not they land major deals. The relationships, the professional network, the experiences, and the lessons they gain from NIL opportunities go far beyond the financial aspect and will carry them into the next season of their lives.

The vast majority of college athletes will not go pro, but even then, the NIL experience is still incredibly valuable. The relationships and networks they build, the resilience they develop, and the lessons they learn will all contribute to their personal and professional growth.

Most importantly, these NIL experiences build their sense of self-worth and provide a perspective that goes beyond the game. They become tools that will help them navigate life's challenges with confidence and a sense of purpose. As a parent, you already know that your child is so much more than just a player in a game. NIL empowers them to discover this truth for themselves and lay the foundation for success that will endure well beyond their time on the field.

CHAPTER TEN

VALUES AND ALIGNMENT

YOUR VALUES ARE the pillars that your personal platform stands on. For parents and their student athletes, the process of clarifying your core values is foundational to your platform, but it doesn't need to be overly scientific. It can be challenging to identify your core values if you're starting from scratch, so I recommend looking at a list of values to see what triggers your intuition. Consider the following core values put together by James Clear. Which ones are particularly important to you?

List of Core Values

AUTHENTICITY, ACHIEVEMENT, ADVENTURE, AUTHORITY, AUTONOMY,

BALANCE, BEAUTY, BOLDNESS, COMPASSION, CHALLENGE, CITIZENSHIP,

COMMUNITY, COMPETENCY, CONTRIBUTION, CREATIVITY, CURIOSITY,

DETERMINATION, FAIRNESS, FAITH, FAME, FRIENDSHIPS, FUN, GROWTH,

HAPPINESS, HONESTY, HUMOR, INFLUENCE, INNER HARMONY, JUSTICE, KINDNESS, KNOWLEDGE, LEADERSHIP, LEARNING, LOVE, LOYALTY, MEANINGFUL WORK, OPENNESS, OPTIMISM, PEACE, PLEASURE, POISE, POPULARITY, RECOGNITION, RELIGION, REPUTATION, RESPECT, RESPONSIBILITY, SECURITY, SELF-RESPECT, SERVICE, SPIRITUALITY, STABILITY, SUCCESS, STATUS, TRUSTWORTHINESS, WEALTH, WISDOM[6]

Circle about ten values that feel right to you. This is your gut check, and it's a good way to reconnect with what you intuitively know about yourself, your unique gifts, and your life experiences. Which of these values speaks to you?

Once you've circled your top ten, it's time to reflect and determine which three or four of these values are absolutely non-negotiable. These are the values that you are unwilling to compromise on because they are integral to who you are and what you hold dear. They represent the essence of your core values.

This exercise is helpful not just for individuals but also for couples and families. I suggest that you and your spouse start by identifying your personal core values independently. It's important to recognize that your values may not align perfectly with your spouse's, and that's okay. In fact, this difference can lead to deeper conversations and greater understanding between you.

The goal is to then come together and, as a couple, define the core values that will guide your family. These family values may not perfectly overlap with your individual values, but they should complement each other and reflect the shared principles that you want to instill in your children.

VALUES AND ALIGNMENT

Why is this exercise so important? Beyond fostering better communication and alignment within the family, your personal core values become a barometer for decision-making, as well as a measuring stick for how you prioritize your time, energy, talent, attention, words, and gifts. They help you identify behaviors or activities that may currently be part of your life but aren't in alignment with what you truly believe is most important. Your personal core values are useful for determining whether you are living your life with integrity or out of alignment.

Indeed, an alignment between values and actions is key to living a life that feels authentic and fulfilling, both for you and your family. Your core values and alignment create the scaffolding to support your growth and ground you in your foundation. You don't want to be out of alignment before you pile on top. Family values also provide another layer of stability. Coming together around family values provides a sense of belonging to something greater, something that transcends individual decision-making.

This sense of connection is something our children often find in sports, where they contribute to a team, play under a banner they deeply resonate with, and feel part of something larger than themselves. Family values can deepen this connection by offering a more profound sense of belonging and a visual, permanent representation of their purpose.

As parents, instilling these values in our children is one of the greatest gifts we can give them. These values serve as conversation starters and pillars that strengthen the bond between parent and child, even as the child grows and eventually leaves home. By referencing these values repeatedly, children develop a deeper, more conscious connection to their roots while spreading their wings.

Family values also offer children a tangible reminder of who they are, not just as athletes but as human beings with inherent value. They are supported, loved, and belong to something meaningful. But these values are not just for the children. They are a gift for parents too. They help us understand where we should invest our time, attention, talents, words, and finances. By regularly reflecting on whether our current choices align with our values, we can identify areas where we may be wasting time or leaving potential untapped.

This act of reflection reveals where we are out of alignment—where we might be wasting talent, energy, or relationships. By understanding our values, we can recapture this potential for growth and redirect it toward more fruitful pursuits.

ASSESSING YOUR VALUES ALIGNMENT

To maximize the benefits of these values, I recommend assessing your values alignment every quarter. Every ninety days, sit down and review your calendar, habits, and how you're spending your time so you can identify areas that need tweaking and realignment. Make adjustments as needed. As you do this over time, you will find that your potential begins to snowball, gaining momentum and taking flight in ways you might not have previously imagined.

When evaluating NIL opportunities, it's important to measure them against your values. This is particularly important because building a brand in the NIL space is not just about marketability but creating something that truly represents who you are and what you stand for. To participate successfully in NIL, you need to intentionally build your brand and platform, both of which hinge on two fundamental elements: your core values and the audience you serve.

Remember: Your brand is not about you. It's about who you serve and what makes you stand out, and your core values represent the unique way you bring your gifts to the table to serve them. Success in NIL hinges on this understanding. Your brand must be deeply rooted in your core values, and these values must resonate with and contribute to the lives of those you aim to serve. You can monetize but don't idolize your brand. It's the basis for your service toward *others*.

When it comes to discussing family values, start with self-reflection and alignment within the family, but ground the discussion in the reality of the fast-paced, ever-changing world our children face. Merely stating, "These are our core values," isn't enough. Your child will encounter daily challenges where their values will be questioned, and it's in these moments that their true understanding of these values will be tested.

Your child will meet friends, teammates, and even teachers who don't share the same values, choices, or goals. Some of these individuals will align closely with your child's values and share similar aspirations and outlooks. But many others won't. These moments of misalignment present opportunities for your child to refine their understanding of their core values.

These values are called "core" for a reason. They are meant to remain steadfast, even when tested. Before your child can discern who supports them, who opposes them, or who is merely misaligned, they must first have a clear sense of who they are. Even then, they must be prepared for their core values to be continually tested throughout their lives. This ongoing testing is what builds resilience, strength, and a sturdy resolve in their beliefs.

YOUR CHILDREN ARE NOT YOU

> *[Your child] is going to decide whether*
> *they want to be great or not.*
> *You can drill them to death,*
> *make them do X,*
> *make them do Y;*
> *You can teach them all these different things.*
> *But when they get older, they're going to decide…*
> *You can't decide that for them.*
> —DAVID POLLACK, COLLEGE FOOTBALL HALL OF FAMER

As parents, while we wish to instill our family values in our children, it's important to also accept that they are not carbon copies of ourselves. This realization often becomes evident when we identify our core values, as we discover that our children may hold different values than we do. After all, they are growing up in a world that is vastly different from the one we experienced. But here's the thing: Your children are meant to be their own individuals with their own light to shine.

We must avoid the temptation of projecting our unfulfilled ambitions or unresolved identities onto our children. They do not need to be burdened with the expectation to achieve what we wish we had in our past or to follow the exact path we took, whether in sports or other areas of life. Our role is not to impose our scorecard on them or dictate their worth. Instead, we must recognize their inherent value and support them as they discover their own path.

We need to strike a delicate balance: instilling family values while allowing children the space to figure things out on their own. Family values should not be wielded as a weapon

VALUES AND ALIGNMENT

or used as a rigid measuring stick. Rather, they should be seen as conversation starters and a gateway to deeper connection. Your goal is to model these values through your actions while offering guidance and support without imposing or lecturing. This is an approach that will contribute to a stronger, more meaningful bond with your children as they learn to make their way in the world.

You will have a far greater impact on your children if you serve as a role model who embodies family values rather than simply delivering lectures on what it means to uphold them. Children learn primarily by observing how you live out your values every day, so focus on trying to consistently practice those values. When you live authentically according to your principles, your children are more likely to internalize your values in a way that feels natural and genuine. This is how family values become an internalized source of strength and guidance, not just a set of rules to follow.

Children learn by watching their parents, often without any explicit instruction. This continues to hold true even as they grow into young adults. They are constantly watching and learning from us, and no one will ever replace parents as the most significant leaders in their lives.

Our role is to engage in meaningful conversations and lead by example, not by using family values as a tool for discipline but by authentically living those values ourselves. It's not about using a "carrot-and-stick" approach to shape their behavior but being a role model who exemplifies the values we hope to instill in them.

So **we instill family values by living them authentically.** It's a challenging task, but it's what's required of us as parents.

THE MOST COMPLEX DECISIONS

Sometimes, you look back and realize that a decision didn't turn out as expected, even though it seemed like the right thing to do at the time. Perhaps you didn't anticipate certain consequences, or maybe you tried something that simply didn't work. This process of reflection and learning is part of maturing. It's how we grow, develop wisdom, and gain perspective.

While undesirable outcomes or obstacles can often be overcome with time and effort, the emotional toll—such as hurt, pride, or regret—is usually temporary. Most poor choices can be corrected relatively quickly in the grand scheme of things. However, the decisions you make about people—how you treat them, who you choose to surround yourself with, and how you allow yourself to be treated—carry a deeper and more lasting impact. These decisions are often not clear-cut or black-and-white. They exist in a gray area where right and wrong are not easily defined. However, you can proactively reflect and reevaluate the deliberately developmental nature of your relationships and surroundings.

The real challenge arises when you make decisions that require you to compromise your values, whether that means letting something slide to avoid offending someone or trying to fit in at the expense of your integrity. These are the moments when your core values must guide you. You need to be clear about who you are and remain steadfast in your values, even when they are tested. This isn't just a challenge for teenagers—it's a lifelong journey that we all must navigate.

The decisions you make regarding people—whether it's setting boundaries, seeking help, or walking away from a relationship that no longer serves your growth and development—are among the most important choices you'll make in life. They can be especially challenging because they involve navigating complex emotions and interpersonal dynamics. However, your core values must still act as a guiding beacon, helping you make these tough decisions with clarity so you surround yourself with growth-oriented, supportive relationships.

Your core values will play a pivotal role in creating a deliberately developmental environment. In such an environment, relationships shouldn't be stagnant but evolving, with everyone committed to growth. Because we're complex human beings, our relationships won't always be perfect. However, they can serve as powerful growth levers to better understand ourselves and differing perspectives at the same time.

Decisions about places, things, or physical choices can often be course-corrected with relative ease, but the decisions you make about relationships—how you treat others and how you allow yourself to be treated—carry a much more significant emotional weight and are harder to reverse if made without careful consideration of your values.

REAL-LIFE DECISION-MAKING MOMENTS

So let's explore some real-life scenarios where a student athlete's sense of values and alignment will be critical for their decision-making.

Of course, one of the first major decisions for any collegiate student athlete is choosing where to attend school. This decision is far more complicated than simply picking a place to play their sport. They also need to find an environment that offers a deliberate developmental growth opportunity.

To help with this decision, many athletes use what's known as the *broken-leg test*. This test poses a simple but profound question: "Would you still want to attend this school if you broke your leg and could no longer play your sport?" In other words, if you had to remove the sport from the equation, would you still be excited about the school, the campus, and the overall environment?

This question cuts to the heart of what you value outside of sports and helps ensure that your choice of school aligns with your broader values and goals. It's a quick and effective way to assess whether a school is truly the right fit.

Beyond selecting a school, student athletes face numerous other decisions that require a strong sense of values. For example, they must carefully choose how they're going to spend their limited downtime and who they spend it with, both within the team and outside of it. The company they keep can significantly influence their experiences and choices, so it's incredibly important that they surround themselves with friends who share and support their values.

Dating is another critical area of decision-making. While parents often discuss who their children should date, they might not focus as much on *how* they date. In today's world, with the prevalence of social media and dating apps, the landscape has shifted dramatically. A student athlete with a clear understanding of their core values will approach dating differently than someone who lacks that clarity. The decision to engage in a meaningful relationship versus casual, transactional ones can have a lasting impact on their emotional well-being and personal growth.

Communication is another area where values play a significant role. Every day, student athletes must make decisions about how they communicate with teammates, coaches, and others. Are they being clear and intentional, or are they avoiding difficult conversations by ghosting people? A student athlete

VALUES AND ALIGNMENT

who values integrity will choose to make that tough phone call or have that difficult conversation rather than leave things unresolved.

Then there's the matter of NIL student athletes, who have the power to decide how they present themselves and what they associate their name and image with. This is where a strong sense of values becomes invaluable. If there are product categories that don't align with your beliefs, it's important to be clear about not promoting them, even if the financial incentive is tempting.

Personally, I wouldn't endorse junk food, even if a company like Frito Lay offered me a substantial sum to promote their products. Such an endorsement wouldn't align with my personal core values or beliefs, and it certainly wouldn't serve the best interests of the people I aim to support. Whether your audience consists of young fans, hometown supporters, business partnerships, or even your future family, the decisions you make now about what you promote and associate with should be a true reflection of your values.

Remember: Above all, your core values are the pillars that guide how you prioritize your time, attention, energy, talents, and the decisions you make about your name, image, and likeness. Every decision, whether you're choosing a school, selecting friends, navigating relationships, communicating with others, or making endorsement deals, should be aligned with your values. It's about staying true to who you are so your actions reflect the values you hold dear.

CHAPTER ELEVEN

RELATIONSHIPS

PERSONAL GROWTH DOESN'T happen in a vacuum. It doesn't come from merely reading self-help books or watching TED talks in isolation. Real transformative growth comes primarily from two things: taking action and engaging in relationships. In fact, relationships are the greatest lever for growth.

The truth is, you can't transform your life without transforming your relationships. They are deeply interconnected with every aspect of your personal development. Self-growth isn't just about working on your mindset or belief structures in isolation. Your full potential and the most joyful, fulfilled version of your life will not be realized unless you are actively engaged in deliberate, developmental relationships that drive growth.

Why is that? Well, for one thing, relationships put you to the test. They stretch you through challenges—sometimes difficult, sometimes uplifting—but always in a way that pushes you to grow. They make you see the world differently, help you form new understandings, and encourage you to incorporate perspectives that may be vastly different from your own.

Sometimes, this is the result of learning how to deal with difficult people. But often, it comes from being exposed to those who lift you up, who call you to rise higher, to stretch further, to climb to your next mountaintop. You simply will not fully realize your potential without relationships.

We can connect this to something we talked about earlier in the book: showing up as a leader in today's VUCA (volatile, uncertain, complex, ambiguous) environment. You see, relationships are a key source of opportunity, whether those relationships feel like sunshine or whether they chafe. In fact, both types of relationships hold opportunities for growth and leadership development. The hard truth is that every relationship, whether harmonious or difficult, is a growth lever if you choose to see it that way.

In today's VUCA world, collaboration is greater and more effective than competition. If you want to grow and succeed in this new landscape, collaboration is not just an option but a requirement. The only way forward is to build a collaborative, leveraged ecosystem with your platform. So if you're only focused on winning by making others lose, you'll be left behind.

In this new reality, we need to focus on creating scenarios where everyone involved can win. No one had to lose in order for us to win. On the contrary, real winning today comes from creating relationships and opportunities where losing isn't even a possibility. So if you want to make a bigger impact, you must think deeper about your relationships because your ability to influence and contribute is directly proportional to the depth and breadth of your relationships.

After her record-setting rookie season in the WNBA, fresh off the heels of her illustrious collegiate career with the Iowa Hawkeyes women's basketball team, a reporter asked Indiana

Fever point guard Caitlyn Clark, "What's been your favorite moment so far?"

She didn't refer to smashing records, making history, or being the number one draft pick. She didn't talk about the brand deals or the ESPY award shows. Her response was a brilliant lesson in how to win. When asked about her favorite moment to date, Caitlyn said, "It's the moments that none of you see that I enjoy the most. It's not the basketball. It's the people I get to spend it with."[7]

HOW RELATIONSHIPS LEAD TO GROWTH

So, how are relationships fodder for growth and development? Well, navigating relationships forces you to develop emotional maturity. You learn deeper communication, build clarity, establish trust, and become someone worthy of trust. Relationships test your alignment with your values and vision. They help you recognize when you or someone else is out of alignment or when a relationship no longer serves its purpose. Through all of this, relationships become the ultimate testing ground for personal and leadership growth.

Put another way, relationships are where the real work happens, and the more you invest in them, the greater your potential for growth. Relationships bring more than just emotional maturity, empathy, and consistency. They also offer you a wealth of perspective and access to knowledge you wouldn't have otherwise. They help you make sense of the world and sharpen your decision-making skills.

When you approach the relationships in your life with intentionality and purpose, the rewards are profound because those relationships become fertile ground for growth. They offer constant feedback, whether verbal or nonverbal, that helps you assess the health and direction of the relationship. This feedback then encourages you to either improve the relationship or, if necessary, make a decision about whether it still serves you.

Gary Vaynerchuk captured this idea perfectly when he said, "People are the ROI of life." That phrase resonated powerfully with me because it neatly summarizes what I've been saying for years about the correlation between impact and relationships. The more you invest in your relationships, the more exponential your impact becomes. If people truly are the return on investment in life, are you investing wisely?

This applies particularly well to student athletes, especially elite college athletes, who are uniquely positioned to cultivate deep, meaningful, and aligned relationships. Our elite student athletes have unparalleled access to future partners, teammates, and peers who can significantly impact their growth and future success. So it's especially important for them to be intentional about building relationships during their time as athletes. By doing so, they can form long-term, mutually beneficial relationships with like-minded individuals.

Student athletes are constantly surrounded by other elite athletes, and among them are people who share similar goals and values. Building relationships with these teammates and peers can lead to powerful connections that extend well beyond the playing field. Additionally, student athletes have access to top-tier coaches—experts in mental performance, skilled trainers, and mentors—who can offer guidance and help them grow both on and off the field. Cultivating these relationships is key to maximizing their development and future opportunities.

But it's not just about coaches and teammates. Athletes are also in a unique position to build meaningful, long-term relationships with their parents as partners on the journey. As parents, you play a critical role in supporting and aligning with your child's goals. This partnership doesn't have to end when their sports career does. It can continue to grow and evolve in a way that benefits both the athlete and the family for years to come. During this relatively brief window of time when your student athlete is participating in college sports, they have the opportunity to deepen these relationships and set the stage for continued growth beyond their athletic career.

Additionally, student athletes often have access to institutional and organizational resources that are designed to support both their athletic and personal development. Whether it's an advisor, a counselor, or even an entrepreneur-in-residence, these resources are available to help them thrive. However, they must be intentional about engaging with these relationships and resources. If they don't invest in them, they'll miss out on a short-term opportunity that could yield significant long-term benefits.

THE VALUE OF A THIRD PERSON

One of the most critical relationships student athletes can develop is with a mentor. Mentors serve as a guiding force that helps them navigate both their personal and professional lives. In the same way that Starbucks has become a "third place" for many people—a comfortable spot between home and work—mentors provide a "third space" of support and wisdom for our students, offering them insight and encouragement as they journey through life and their careers.

Every sports family needs someone—a "third person," as it were—to fill the role of confidant, mentor, or guide. While no one will ever replace a parent as the primary leader in their child's life, having a third person who shares the family's values and vision creates a vital support system for student athletes. The outside perspective of this mentor, rather than being a competing voice, acts as a partner to the parents. In fact, a good mentor will help reinforce the values parents have instilled and provide an additional layer of support.

Just like a sturdy stool requires three legs, this third support provides stability and balance. Practically speaking, a mentor does this by acting as a sounding board that can offer guidance without the emotional weight or expectations that often come from the parent-child relationship. Their role is to help the student stay on their path, aligned with their purpose, so they can achieve the next level of growth.

Just as a coffee shop like Starbucks provides a "third place" to relax and refocus between our personal and professional lives, a mentor offers a neutral, supportive environment where goals and vision can be revisited without the pressures of family dynamics. Athletes can bounce ideas off a mentor and receive feedback and encouragement that may be difficult to get from a parent who is deeply invested in the outcome. In a way, the mentor's value lies in their impartiality because they are a third party who is committed to the growth and development of the young leader but without the emotional baggage that sometimes complicates family conversations.

For sports families, having this third voice can be a game changer. The mentor doesn't replace the parent or diminish their influence. They simply add an additional layer of stability and wisdom that keeps the young athlete focused on their goals and purpose, helping to guide them through the unique challenges and opportunities of their journey.

JENNY WEAST: AN INVINCIBLE SUMMER

I understand the impact of a mentor because of my own experience with my "third person" during a pivotal stage in my personal development. Her name was Jenny Weast, but we called her "Weaster." She was someone who poured into me during my formative years and truly became a guide, mentor, and inspiration for me.

If I had to describe Jenny in one word, that word would be "up." Jenny spent her life showing me the way up—stretching me, pushing me to grow and surpass my own expectations. What makes her story even more remarkable is that Jenny spent her own life looking up. You see, at the age of sixteen, she suffered a tragic skiing accident that left her a quadriplegic and wheelchair-bound for the rest of her life. From that moment on, she had no choice but to look up to her coworkers, caregivers, students, and friends. But more than that, Jenny was someone who never gave up. She never let her circumstances define her or hold her back.

Jenny was my cheerleading coach. Yes, you heard that right—a quadriplegic cheerleading coach. People were often stunned to find out that she had won championship cheerleading trophies and mentored dance and cheer athletes for nearly thirty years. But more than the trophies, what truly defined Jenny was her grit. She faced her challenges head-on and, in a remarkable turn of events, even returned to ski the very mountain where she had her accident forty years earlier. She navigated that mountain in a specially designed sled and skied down the same slopes that had taken her physical abilities but could never take her spirit.

One of Jenny's favorite quotes was from Albert Camus: "In the midst of winter, I found within me an invincible summer." Jenny lived this quote every day. She taught me, and so many others, what it means to find that invincible summer within ourselves. Jenny was not just my coach but my mentor and my friend. She impacted thousands of young athletes, parents, friends, and colleagues with her resilience, her positive spirit, and her unwavering commitment to living life to its fullest.

Despite the odds stacked against her, Jenny lived at her personal edge, pushing herself—and everyone around her—forward. She created environments where each individual felt empowered and invincible, just as she did. As a coach, she moved teams into winning circles, collecting trophies and accolades year after year. But the thing she cherished most wasn't the awards or recognition but the relationships she built, the connections that lifted her up and allowed her to keep growing, both as a person and a leader.

Jenny Weaster embodied a warrior mentality. She was always in action, deliberately investing her time and energy into other people. Though her physical body was disabled, she lived like a lighthouse in the darkness, showing others how to conquer their own mountains while lifting them up at scale. Jenny made relationships her mission, not by getting on stages, giving seminars, or even using a megaphone as a cheer coach. Instead, she lifted each person up, one personal relationship at a time. One by one, she built people up with her unwavering presence and spirit. She built her platform, her people, and her ecosystem up so that long-term success and a winning impact was inevitable. She got the momentum rolling (pun intended; she would like that joke) and became an unstoppable force for good.

It wasn't until her funeral in March of 2022 that I truly realized the massive scale of her impact. Her relationships and investment in others filled the old high school gymnasium to standing room only. Alumni, teachers, friends, family, and even parents of alumni came to pay their respects and celebrate her life.

As speaker after speaker took the stage, they all shared the same lessons that Jenny had instilled in me as my mentor. Each person had a unique story about how Jenny had encouraged them and how she had lifted them up, but the underlying message was the same. She showed them what they were capable of, just as she had done for me. She helped people see their unique gifts and talents, and she did this not only through her words but by living her life as an example.

Her life was full of joy and adventure, and she was always ready to rise up and meet challenges, always ready to face adversity. I had the privilege of seeing a side of her that few others did. I saw her in her most vulnerable moments, facing setbacks—physically and financially—that came with lifelong caregiving dependencies. Even then, she showed up for others. She remained a role model, a true friend, and a beacon of resilience.

Jenny was a uniquely gifted leader. But here's the thing: You, too, have the potential to lead in a way that moves others forward. Like Jenny, you can *choose* to be someone who never quits, never settles, and always strives to live with integrity. If anything, I hope her story inspires you to maximize your own potential and the potential of those around you, in your family, your community, and your circles of influence.

Jenny's legacy endures as a powerful reminder that true leadership comes not from avoiding challenges but from facing them with courage, resilience, and a heart full of gratitude for the relationships that help us rise above. She lived her life full out, and her story continues to inspire me to do the same. I hope it inspires you, too.

A STEADY PILLAR FOR YOUR STUDENT ATHLETE

A great mentor plays a unique role in keeping you and your student athlete on the path of greater purpose, even when external circumstances are chaotic and uncertain. In today's tumultuous world, having a mentor who not only understands and believes in you but also helps you navigate through challenging times is invaluable.

Unlike other relationships, a mentor serves as a steady pillar. They provide stability and offer guidance and support when everything else feels unpredictable. While friends, colleagues, and even family may offer encouragement or advice, a mentor helps anchor you to your purpose so you stay aligned with your long-term goals, even when distractions or challenges arise.

In this sense, a mentor is not just a supportive figure but a constant, sturdy presence that helps you weather the storms of life. They offer perspective, wisdom, and a steady hand when the external world feels like it's spiraling out of control. And that's what sets a mentor apart from other relationships: They serve as a compass, always guiding you back to your true north, no matter how far off course you may feel.

And that's why mentorship is at the heart of what we do at NIL Builders Group. The personal relationships, facilitating peer-to-peer conversations, and cultivating a supportive environment is what sets us apart from other NIL coaching or education courses. If you want to see how we can support

RELATIONSHIPS

your athlete and your family through this exciting developmental time in their lives, use this QR code, or visit www.nilbuildersgroup.com.

CHAPTER TWELVE

WHAT DOES SUCCESS LOOK LIKE?

THROUGHOUT THIS BOOK, we've talked about the various strategies that will help your student athlete achieve success—from building relationships and finding a great mentor to defining your values and aligning your decisions to them, from setting long-term goals to making the most of NIL opportunities. But what does success actually look like? What does it look like for student athletes, and just as importantly, what does it look like for *you*, the parent of a student athlete?

This is such an important question because success, while deeply personal, often requires distinct perspectives for both groups. Let's tackle each one.

SUCCESS FOR PARENTS

For parents, to use the Jedi metaphor we introduced earlier, success is like being Yoda to your child's Luke Skywalker. In other words, it's about seeing your young leader hit their stride, watching them grow, stretch, and reach their potential. It's about witnessing your child accelerate their gifts, build character, gain confidence, and tackle challenges with grace, grit, and determination.

Ultimately, as parents, we want to see our children win at life, don't we? Not just in the short term but with a long-term perspective that sets them up for sustained success. Speaking personally, my goal is for my children to grow into the leaders they were meant to be, embracing their gifts and potential and stepping into their own unique path, equipped to serve others and find peace and prosperity despite the swirling winds of change they'll face.

SUCCESS FOR STUDENT ATHLETES

For student athletes, success often takes on a different meaning, particularly in the short window of time when they are actively pursuing their athletic and academic careers. Their definition of success might involve increasing their influence, securing NIL deals, gaining new opportunities, or standing out in their sport to build momentum for future success. Many student athletes are already thinking beyond their athletic accomplishments and starting to pave the way for life after graduation. They want to feel like they're in their flow, gaining confidence, building their skill set, and ultimately succeeding both on and off the field.

Between parents and student athletes, there's a shared theme: continuous improvement. For both, the journey never really ends. Just as parents see their children grow and develop their potential, student athletes must recognize that their goals and metrics for success will continue to evolve as they mature. The most successful people, whether they are student athletes or leaders in other fields, realize that their potential is limitless, and because of that, they are never done reaching for more.

Persistence, consistency, and success build momentum over time, but at the same time, you must stay humble along the way. The real danger for any successful high performer, whether a student or adult, is complacency. It's easy to start thinking, *I've made it*, or, *This is good enough*, but that mindset is where most leaders stumble. The moment hubris creeps in, when you start thinking your past success guarantees future stability, that is often the point where the world throws a curveball to wake you up. True leaders, however, are humbled by these experiences and reignited to continue learning and growing.

On the other hand, those who stop reaching, who become comfortable with their level of success, often see their greatness start to fade. Mediocrity is where greatness goes to die, not because of external setbacks but because of self-inflicted stagnation. If you stop striving, stop growing, that's where progress halts. As morbid as it might sound, if you're not growing, you're dying. Continuous growth, in both mindset and action, is essential to long-term success. This is a lesson that applies not only to student athletes but to leaders at any stage of their journey.

If you stop reaching for growth, learning, or greatness, that's when you begin to stagnate. Your potential starts to atrophy, and your greatness begins to wane. When this happens, life has a way of sending a wake-up call as a reminder that none of us are here to be basic or average. We are here to shine, to share our unique gifts, and to positively impact others. And so, the work isn't done as long as we're still breathing.

The most successful people understand this. They embrace a continuous improvement model because they know they're never finished. That's why they remain humble and always striving for more.

A CHANGING DEFINITION OF SUCCESS

As we achieve goals and milestones, our definition of success is eventually going to change. The reason for this is twofold. First, you are going to evolve as a leader. As you do, you gain perspective and elevate to new levels, and your goals and priorities shift. While your core values and innate gifts remain unchanged, how you use them may evolve.

Second, the world is constantly turning. The rapid rate of change isn't slowing down. It's here to stay, and what's more? The rate is accelerating. Circumstances and opportunities will change as the world spins on, and that's why it's so vital to embrace change rather than fear it. Leading through change means recognizing that your potential to grow, lift others, and serve will continuously shift. The way you deliver your talents and influence may change, but your potential remains massive. Like so many things, this is true for both student athletes and parents.

By building a stable platform to stand on, you will amplify your impact, which will allow you to reach even more people and have a greater positive influence. And the more you can adapt to the ever-changing landscape around you, the more you'll be able to make use of the opportunities that arise.

I understand this from firsthand experience because I had to learn how to redefine my own success after my NFL pro cheerleading career ended. I actually retired twice. The first retirement was forced on me after my rookie season. I wasn't selected to return to the team, and it blindsided me. I had no real feedback, no clear reason why. Despite feeling shocked and frustrated, I knew I wasn't done. I still had more to give, and I wanted another shot.

So, I got into action. I decided that in the next audition season, I would be so good they couldn't ignore me. I put my head down, became laser-focused, and prioritized everything that would make me a stronger athlete. I did my research, trained harder, and leveled up in every way I could. And it worked.

I came back, not just for one more season but for three. I served as captain for two of those seasons, and one year, we even made it to the Super Bowl (Super Bowl XLIII: Pittsburgh Steelers versus Arizona Cardinals). I was also selected for the military show team and traveled overseas to perform for our troops. Through that perseverance and determination, I found silver linings and built relationships that I wouldn't have otherwise.

That was my comeback story, a story of resilience, of being tested and sticking with it. But my real retirement came later, and this time it was my choice. After four successful seasons with the NFL, I was ready to hang up my pom-poms. By then, I was thirty years old, married, with a graduate degree, and ready to dive into new chapters of building a career and investing in my personal life.

Even though it was my decision, retiring still hit me hard. The loss of identity, the shock of closing a chapter that had been decades in the making, was something I wrestled with for months. No longer was there a mandatory workout schedule or practices to attend. There were no more team gatherings, no opportunities to catch up with friends and teammates regularly.

For the first time, I was on my own, without the structure I'd relied on for so long. It wasn't easy to adjust, and it took time to redefine what success looks like for me in this new phase of life. But that's the nature of growth. Just when you think you've figured it all out, life shifts, and you're called to step up again, to embrace new challenges, and to keep moving forward.

NAVIGATING A SEASON OF TRANSITION

As my career shifted and my time as an NFL cheerleader came to an end, I found myself in a season of transition. Some of the deep relationships I had built during that time remained, but others faded away. Despite having mentally prepared for the end of my cheerleading days, the reality of the shift still hit hard. It felt like I was entering a winter season in my life.

I remember feeling a deep sense of loss as I packed away my practice gear, the team posters, the boots, and the game-day makeup. Questions kept running through my mind: *Who am I now? Who am I without this identity?*

Fortunately, those seeds I had been planting outside of NFL cheerleading also began to sprout, and I had something to turn to. I was able to dive into entrepreneurship, sports business, and marketing, and nurture the communities and relationships I had built outside of my NFL career. In this, I was very fortunate. Not all of my peers had something to turn to when their time on the field was over.

This experience taught me an important lesson: Never attach your entire identity to a team, a company, a sport, or a brand. Nothing in this world is guaranteed, and when you define yourself by just one thing, you risk losing your sense of self when it's taken away. What's most important is to stay connected to who you are at your core and remain in alignment with that. When you are grounded in your true self, you can weather the different seasons of life with resilience.

WHAT DOES SUCCESS LOOK LIKE?

What initially felt like a setback—my own winter season—turned out to be the launchpad for new opportunities. It was as if my life was a slingshot, being pulled back only to be catapulted forward. That period of loss made space for the next chapter of my life, one that allowed me to invest more of my time, attention, and talents into areas that had been waiting in the wings.

And now, fifteen years removed from my NFL career, my perspective has shifted. Success used to be measured by external achievements, but now it is much more internal. As a mother and mentor to emerging leaders, I feel more compelled than ever to invest in others, sharing the wisdom I've gained along the way. Now, I work with several current NFL and collegiate teams to train on leadership development in what feels like a true full-circle moment.

Success, for me, is no longer about the glitter and excitement of game day. It's about deepening relationships and feeling aligned with my purpose. The glitter eyeshadow may have faded, but what remains is a higher calling that brings even more joy than cheering for touchdowns. Watching my family grow and seeing how my career and personal investments have blossomed is how I know I'm on the right path.

ENTERING THE NEXT CHAPTER OF LIFE

For student athletes and their parents, the tools and tactics they've learned in sports can be incredibly valuable as they enter the next chapter of life. Sports teach discipline, perseverance, and the importance of teamwork—skills that are transferable to any career or life endeavor.

However, it's important to recognize that success isn't just about mastering technical or tactical skills. Technical skills acquisition is often referred to in human development as "horizontal growth." Horizontal growth is about acquiring new abilities, like you did throughout your sports career, and leveling up your expertise. As you transition beyond sports, what's even more important is *vertical growth*.

Vertical growth is about developing life skills, character, and leadership. It's about taking what you've learned on the field—discipline, resilience, and adaptability—and applying it to your personal and professional life in a way that deepens your impact. Your platform works to amplify your ability to be a force for good. It's this vertical growth that will carry you through the transitions in life and help you continue to evolve your platform and as a leader.

No matter what chapter of life you're in, you are meant to keep growing, both horizontally by acquiring new skills and vertically by deepening your character and relationships. This growth, especially the vertical kind, is what will allow you to thrive beyond the playing field and achieve long-lasting success.

In fact, throughout this book, I've been focused primarily on vertical growth, encouraging you and your student athletes to cultivate inner agility, resilience, and adaptive skills while increasing your capacity to face challenges and embrace change. This culminates in vertical growth, and it's impossible to achieve alone.

THE ROLE OF FAITH

What's truly fascinating is what happens when you combine both horizontal and vertical growth. Together, these two forms of growth create a powerful balance, and visually, they form a cross. This connection between horizontal and vertical development serves as a metaphor for our lives—a path of constant learning and evolving with a higher purpose guiding us toward where we should focus our energy and attention.

And that brings us to the role of faith. You see, faith is something that helps us maintain a firm foundation through life's transitions. Faith isn't just an isolated belief but the foundation upon which all other structures and activities are built. Faith gives you the stability to continue growing both horizontally and vertically. It supports upward mobility and allows you to increase your capacity for growth and achievement while also grounding you in something unshakeable.

In a world that is constantly changing and accelerating, faith becomes the immovable rock that provides the principles and strength to weather any storm. It's the harbor you can return to when storms arise. With faith, you're able to plant roots deep in the ground, even as you grow.

This firm foundation allows you to reach new heights while staying connected to something greater than yourself. Faith, in this sense, is the anchor that keeps you steady as you navigate life's inevitable transitions and challenges, and it gives you the confidence to keep moving forward.

CONCLUSION

THANKS FOR TAKING this journey with me. Hopefully, it's just the beginning. However, I'd like to share a final word of encouragement for all those parents who want to sponsor the greatness in their kids—who want to encourage, empower, fund, and see that greatness come to fruition.

Remember: Above all, how you show up for your child is of the utmost importance. As a parent, you are their guide. You're not there to do the work for them or dictate their path but to place them in environments that deliberately challenge and develop their skills. Your children are going to face tests, and they *need* to face them. Your role is to encourage that growth, empower their efforts, and invest in experiences that are designed to bring out their full potential.

Be intentional about where you invest your time and resources in their development. Seek out the kinds of environments that will help them stretch their abilities and grow into the greatness they are capable of. My call to action for all parents is simple: Elevate your own game by lifting up your children. Sponsor your child's journey by placing them in an ecosystem that fosters winning scenarios.

If you really want your kids to step into their full potential, their impact, and their influence, you have to give them the opportunity to rise to challenges. But it's not just about the individual test. They also need to learn to collaborate and work with others because relationships are going to play a pivotal role in their long-term success. They need experiences where they put their skills to use not just for their own benefit but in service of others. This is where true greatness lies—building their talents and character to help others grow as well.

I believe this is critically important for both parents and students to understand: The investment in building up character isn't just about making your child stronger for their own sake. Character development is about strengthening their capacity to lift *others* up. Sure, resilience and adaptability are going to help them face their challenges, but it doesn't stop there.

The growth of character is meant to be a platform from which they can reach down and help others rise to meet *their* challenges as well. In other words, it's about progressing toward their own goals while also reaching back to help people who can benefit from their unique talents and support.

Intentionally creating an environment that will foster this kind of growth means seeking out mentors, peer groups, like-minded parents, and support systems that can guide not only the student athlete but the entire sports family through their journey. The payoff for doing this is significant. By sponsoring your athlete's greatness and guiding them into developmental experiences, you're setting them up to thrive in the ever-changing world.

As parents, you have the power to be intentional in shaping the future for your children. And in doing so, you're helping them not only to grow but to lead, influence, and positively impact the world around them.

CONCLUSION

We're Ready to Help

My team and I are fully committed to helping families navigate this new VUCA landscape called college athletics. We offer mentorship and opportunities for student athletes to build their platform and character deliberately and intentionally. You can learn more at our website and schedule a free personal strategy call for you and your athlete with my team: www.nilbuildersgroup.com

Ultimate Winning Season—Bonus Resources

Now that you have the context for creating your family's vision, it's time to jumpstart your journey together with your athlete. I'd like to share bonus materials with you that are exclusively for Ultimate Winning Season readers. These resources and tools help you to hit the ground running with your own personalized NIL strategy, while strengthening your family connection at the same time.

Get your Free downloads of the *Ultimate Winning Season Discussion Guide*, my curated list of Ultimate NIL tools, resources, news sources, and subject matter experts in the space, and most importantly, *The Ultimate Winning Season—Student Athlete Guidebook*, to assist your athlete in learning to own their opportunity in NIL.

Download the free bonus materials and schedule a free personal strategy call for you and your athlete now at www.ultimatewinningseason.com/resources.

ULTIMATE WINNING SEASON— READER'S GUIDE

INTRODUCTION

KEY TAKEAWAYS
- **Embrace Change as Opportunity:**
  Change is inevitable and accelerating, especially in the world of college athletics. By approaching it with an open mind and proactive attitude, parents can position themselves and their children to thrive amid uncertainty.
- **The Parent as Mentor-Leader:**
  Parents are essential guides during their children's transitions into adulthood. This role requires evolving alongside their children, committing to personal growth, and cultivating adaptability to navigate challenges together.
- **Winners Versus Spinners:**
  Those who adapt and take decisive action despite uncertainty ("winners") can thrive in a VUCA (Volatile, Uncertain, Complex, Ambiguous) environment, while those who hesitate or get overwhelmed ("spinners") risk falling behind.

- **Growth Through the Changes:**
  Personal growth is necessary for effective parental support during this critical life transition for you and for your athlete.

DISCUSSION QUESTIONS

1. In what ways can you model adaptability, optimism, and growth for your child as they face the fast-changing landscape of college athletics and life?
2. In what ways are you positively showing up for your family as a parent-leader? In what ways are you currently *not* showing up at your highest level?
3. Was there a time in your life when you related to being a "spinner" and feeling stuck? What were the circumstances around that time in your life? In hindsight, what relationships, mindset, or actions did you take that helped you get "unstuck"?
4. Think about a recent challenge you've faced. How did your mindset impact the outcome, and what could you do differently next time to turn the challenge into an opportunity?

ACTION ITEM

Schedule a dedicated, distraction-free conversation with your student athlete to discuss their goals, fears, and expectations for their upcoming athletic and academic journey. Listen more than you speak, and focus on understanding their perspective.

ULTIMATE WINNING SEASON–READER'S GUIDE

CHAPTER ONE: VUCA (VOLATILE, UNCERTAIN, COMPLEX, AND AMBIGUOUS)

KEY TAKEAWAYS

- **Adaptability as a Competitive Advantage:**
"Adaptability means learning how to adjust strategies and behaviors in response to new information and changing circumstances." Adaptability isn't just about reacting to challenges but actively reflecting on how you process your thoughts, emotions, and decisions to respond effectively to change. The ability to adjust to rapid changes in circumstances, whether on the field or in NIL opportunities, is critical to thriving in a VUCA world. Developing self-awareness and flexibility is the foundation for success in uncertain environments.
- **Sense-and-Respond Decision-Making:**
Athletes with inner agility are better equipped to make informed and balanced decisions in the face of imperfect information and ambiguity. Strong decision-making involves sensing and responding to uncertainty while aligning actions with values and long-term goals.
- **The Opportunity in NIL:**
While NIL introduces complexity, it also offers student athletes a unique training ground for building entrepreneurial skills, financial literacy, and personal branding that prepare them for life beyond sports. "The NIL opportunity has opened up a training ground for professional experiences."

DISCUSSION QUESTIONS

1. Do you think that the rate of change is increasing as rapidly as it's made out to be in this chapter? In what areas

of your life are you particularly feeling the effects of the VUCA environment?
2. How comfortable am I with uncertainty and change? Is it possible to live in a world with a brighter future alongside rapid change?
3. Which of the five pillars of inner agility do you naturally lean into? Which one do you see as an opportunity to improve in yourself? The pillars of inner agility are adaptability, improved decision-making, resilience, creativity and innovation, and stronger relationships.
4. Which pillar of inner agility do you think is most critical for your student athlete to develop, and why?

ACTION ITEM
Adopt a mindset of opportunity: Reflect on a current challenge or goal you're working on and where you may begin to see the opportunity hidden in your approach, responses, perception, or outlook on the situation.

CHAPTER TWO: AGILITY FOR THE WIN

KEY TAKEAWAYS
- **Leaders Lean into Challenges by Taking Action**:
  If you go on offense, you'll gain new insights. Distractions pile up when you're operating in reactions.
- **Creativity and Curiosity Are Key to Navigating VUCA Environments**:
  Curiosity unlocks your creativity, which becomes your competitive advantage in a rapidly changing environment.

- **Adaptive Skills:**
  Are Crucial for Long-Term Success beyond Technical Abilities in a Rapidly Changing World.
- **Success Requires a Proactive, Adaptive Leadership Approach:**
  (Action + Agility) x (Growth Mindset + Resilience) = flexibility, responsiveness, and innovation.

DISCUSSION QUESTIONS

1. How can you model a growth mindset and adaptive leadership for your student athlete?
2. What area of your life do you feel you're operating in reactionary mode? What adjustment can you make in the face of that challenge in order to be more flexible and action oriented?
3. How have you already witnessed VUCA impacting your child's athletic journey?
4. How can you help your student athlete transfer their adaptability on the field into other areas of life, such as academics or NIL opportunities?

ACTION ITEM

Use the what-if question to overcome fear and foster curiosity, driving more proactive and innovative thinking. Especially when you're feeling "stuck" or facing a difficult challenge— take a pause to step back from the situation and ask yourself what-if questions. Jot down your thoughts to unlock insights, creativity, and ideas for moving forward.

CHAPTER THREE: RESILIENCE + GROWTH

KEY TAKEAWAYS

- **Growth Mindset Is a Practice:**
  A growth mindset is an ongoing practice, much like training for a championship. It's not an innate trait but a skill that is developed through intentional effort over time.
- **Resilience Unlocks Your Brilliance:**
  Resilience is not just bouncing back from failure—it's about continuously adapting to feedback and learning from mistakes. It's an evolving skill that allows individuals to stay agile and keep moving forward, even when facing setbacks. It's the most critical pillar of inner agility for you and your student athlete to develop in order to ensure your ultimate winning seasons ahead.
- **Feedback as Fuel for Growth:**
  Feedback, whether it's positive or negative, provides the data needed for refinement and progress. Each obstacle, if viewed through a resilient lens, is an opportunity to improve and come back stronger. Use each experience to learn and adjust rather than as a measure of failure.
- **The One-Word Lesson Is "Stick-to-itiveness":**
  Effort outperforms talent in the long game of life. This persistence in the face of adversity is the key to long-term success. If you have stick-to-itiveness, especially in the moments where you're facing setbacks and challenges, you'll cut down on the time you spend ruminating and worrying. The mental shift moves you forward so you can keep taking action no matter what and ultimately win.

- **Parental Role:**
  Parents can model resilience and a growth mindset for their student athletes, guiding them to handle challenges with a constructive, optimistic approach.

DISCUSSION QUESTIONS

1. How can you develop a growth mindset in your daily life, both in terms of work and personal growth?
2. What role does feedback play in your own personal growth? How do you react to feedback in both positive and negative situations?
3. In what ways can you help your student athlete learn to embrace challenges as growth opportunities instead of viewing them as obstacles?
4. Reflect on a recent challenge faced by your child athlete. How could you have better supported them in developing a resilient mindset?

ACTION ITEM

Stick-to-itiveness Reflection Practice: Reflect on one particular challenge or setback you faced where you had to persevere. Write down how you responded and what feedback you can gather from the experience. Then, identify one way to adjust your approach or actions based on the learnings you gained. To put this into practice regularly, block thirty minutes time in your calendar monthly to reflect on your "stick-to-itiveness" practices in the past thirty days. This simple action will help reinforce resilience and growth mindset practices to stay at the top of your awareness for continuous improvement. You can do this monthly reflection as a solo practice or with your family together.

CHAPTER FOUR: TRANSITIONS

KEY TAKEAWAYS
- **Embracing Change:**
  Parents must accept that their role is evolving. This doesn't mean stepping away but shifting from being a decision-maker to a guide. It requires letting go of the past and embracing the new realities of the college environment. Parents must model resilience and support their children in managing stress and making decisions in a fast-paced, interconnected world.
- **GUIDE Framework:**
  A tool for parents to navigate this transition and guide their athletes effectively:
  - **Growth:**
    Encourage a mindset of continuous learning.
  - **Understanding:**
    Know the landscape and rules affecting your child's journey.
  - **Integrity:**
    Lead by example with trustworthiness and strong ethical values.
  - **Direction:**
    Help them stay focused on long-term goals.
  - **Empowerment:**
    Build their confidence and sense of independence.
- **What's Next for Parents:**
  As your child becomes more independent, you may face a shift in your own identity and priorities. With more free time and space comes the opportunity to reevaluate your own growth, passions, and aspirations.

- **Handing Over the Keys:**
  Transitioning from the driver of your child's athletic journey to a partner or contributor is a crucial step in this transition period. Enable your child to take ownership of their path in their life and athletic career by supporting their development without overshadowing their journey. Intentionally model these attributes and actions as a parent-leader yourself, and be deliberate about enabling the developmental environments where your athlete can thrive.

DISCUSSION QUESTIONS

1. As a parent, what new experiences or opportunities are you looking forward to in this period of transition and growth?
2. What are the biggest uncertainties you foresee for your student athlete's future? How can you prepare to help them navigate those challenges?
3. How can you begin to adjust your role from being the primary decision-maker to a supportive mentor in "handing over the keys" to your athlete's journey?
4. How can you empower your student athlete to begin taking more ownership of their decisions?

ACTION ITEM

Agile Parenting Cycle: In your personal and family reflection practices, utilize flexibility through cycles of "Observe, Adapt, Act, Reflect." You can use this cycle to brainstorm and experiment with new ideas to hone in on areas for growth in your existing goals and also to reset or refresh goals or commitments that no longer serve you in this phase of life. Encourage your child to go through this cycle to guide them through their challenges, as well. In this agile practice, you'll use this repeatable cycle:

- Observe—use your what-if curiosity to trigger creative ideas or deeper understanding
- Adapt—the incorporation of past feedback and learnings
- Act—taking a new action or new approach
- Reflect—an intentional pause to capture retrospective insights and feedback that come from your latest cycle of experience

CHAPTER FIVE: THE POWER OF A PLATFORM

KEY TAKEAWAYS

- **Platforms Provide a Powerful Structure** to create value, support activities, and accelerate growth. Building and owning your platform leads to increased impact, influence, and income-generating opportunities while maintaining alignment with your core values and purpose.
- **A Platform Is Essential to Your Success in Two Ways:**
  - **Your platform enables you to lift others up.** It gives you elevation and structure for greater expansion and legacy impact.
  - **Your platform makes it easier to collaborate with others to share your vision,** understand what you stand for and how to work alongside you, and is central to your own decision-making, short-term and long-term growth.

- **Without Pillars, Platforms Crumble:** Make your platform structurally sound by fortifying your foundational core values, principles, and purpose.
- **As a Parent, You Are Building Your Own Platform as a "Life Operating System"** that guides decisions, fosters resilience, and serves as a foundation for long-term success, both for your student athlete and your family.
- **Platforms Accelerate Dynamic Growth:** Your platform evolves with feedback and experience to better adapt and support future opportunities.
- **Platforms Thrive on Purpose. The Platformula Process** is an agile, personalized framework for building a student athlete's brand and business aligned with their purpose to strategically leverage opportunities.

DISCUSSION QUESTIONS

1. What steps do you need to take to build a stronger shared understanding of your family's core values? How can you further model those attributes as a parent?
2. In what ways can building a platform together strengthen your relationship with your student athlete and enhance their long-term potential?
3. How can you use your platform to serve others?

ACTION ITEM

Shared Values—Write down three core values that define your personal platform as a parent. Then, spend time establishing and discussing a shared value set of three to five family values. As a family, identify one specific way you can each embody one family value in the coming week, and repeat the reflection and/or focus on a family value each week.

CHAPTER SIX: THE REAL NIL

KEY TAKEAWAYS
- **See NIL as a Pathway to Leadership and Entrepreneurial Growth**, not just a financial gain. Leverage it to develop character and business acumen.
- **Proactive Mindset:**
  Taking initiative and being strategic in building a personal brand, even for athletes not aiming for professional sports careers, is a critical skill for your athlete to develop.
- **Avoiding "Shiny Object Syndrome":**
  While NIL presents vast opportunities, it's easy to fall into the trap of chasing short-term, flashy offers without a clear vision. This can lead to brand dilution, burnout, overcommitment, and poor decision-making.
- **Managing Risks in NIL:**
  Aggressive marketers and promoters often target student athletes with appealing offers that may compromise their long-term success or safety. It's crucial for athletes to stay focused on their goals and avoid deals that don't align with their vision.
- **Role of Schools in NIL:**
  Many parents mistakenly believe that their child's school will drive their NIL success. In reality, schools can provide valuable support, but student athletes must take charge of their own strategies and opportunities.
- **Parenting in the NIL Era:**
  Just like a parent teaches a child to drive, they must now trust their student athletes to steer their NIL journey. Parents should provide guidance and support but allow their athletes to navigate their own path toward success.

DISCUSSION QUESTIONS

1. What are some signs that a student athlete might be falling victim to shiny object syndrome in the NIL space? How can you facilitate their understanding of what constitutes a good fit versus a misaligned opportunity?
2. How can parents help their children grow in independence while still offering guidance in the NIL landscape?

ACTION STEP

Encourage your athlete to run all potential NIL opportunities through a decision-making filter. This can be a simple checklist:

- Does this align with my brand's values?
- Is this opportunity a short-term gain or a long-term investment?
- What are the risks (time, reputation, resources)?
- Does this align with my larger goals (personal, professional, NIL-related)?

This filter will help them evaluate offers before making commitments.

CHAPTER SEVEN: PLATFORMULA FOR SUCCESS

KEY TAKEAWAYS
- **The Platform Owner's Power Formula (POP):**
Combining perspective, shared vision, collaboration, and clear priorities creates a leveraged and adaptable platform that accelerates growth.

- **Ownership Mindset:**
Success in NIL requires an ownership mindset, where the athlete builds tools, services, and offerings to maximize impact and maintain long-term growth, rather than emotional or short-term reactions.
- **Force Multipliers:**
Collaboration and clear priorities enable exponential growth, aligning actions with the shared vision.
- **Platform Benefits:**
A well-built platform offers leverage, velocity, and value creation, ensuring sustainability and adaptability across various future scenarios.
- **Principles of Platform Building:**
Trust, long-term vision, strategic decisions, and ecosystem enablement form the foundation of a robust platform.
- **Brand Is an Asset, Platform Is the Engine:**
An athlete's NIL brand is an asset tied to reputation, while the platform is the strategic foundation that amplifies and leverages that brand for partnerships, influence, and growth. Your platform is the infrastructure that drives visibility, connections, impact and income.
- **The NIL space** offers real-time opportunities for student athletes and their families, but the focus should be on building a lasting legacy that extends beyond immediate success.
- **The success** of a sports family is enabled by three pillars: **build**, **belong**, and **become**.
  - **Build** emphasizes developing the athlete's brand, business acumen, and platform while also empowering parents to support their athlete's growth.
  - **Belong** highlights the importance of community, networking, and collaboration within a group coaching and mentoring environment.

- **Become** focuses on leadership development, equipping families and athletes with the skills needed to navigate an unpredictable world both in athletics and beyond.
- **Lifting others and serving with your gifts** are fundamental to realizing your full potential.

DISCUSSION QUESTIONS

1. What steps have you taken so far to establish the athlete's personal brand? Are there gaps in these efforts that need attention?
2. How can an athlete separate their NIL brand from their personal identity while still maintaining authenticity in their platform?
3. What role do you see the athlete playing in their broader community as a leader, and how can they use their platform to inspire others?
4. How can you expand your athlete's mentorship network to ensure they are receiving guidance from people who have succeeded in both athletic and entrepreneurial fields?
5. How do you and your athlete currently define success, and how does this align with your long-term vision for their growth in NIL and beyond?
6. How can you actively contribute to building your athlete's personal brand while also developing your own platform to support their growth?
7. How do your actions demonstrate consistency, integrity, and professionalism? In what areas could you build greater trust with partners and collaborators in your efforts?

ACTION ITEM
Participate in an upcoming NIL Builders Workshop to work through these assessments and more with our team to guide you. Learn more and register at nilbuildersgroup.com

SELF-STUDY
Conduct a Platform Owner's Assessment: Using the POP formula, evaluate your current state of platform ownership potential across the four key areas:

- **Perspective:** Identify one area to expand your understanding or network.
- **Shared Vision:** Define or refine your mission statement.
- **Collaboration:** List ten to twenty current or potential partners, mentors, or supporters who align with your vision.
- **Clear Priorities:** Establish one immediate and one long-term priority that aligns with your shared vision. Think of how your actions can start to build trust and demonstrate consistency and integrity toward your mission.

CHAPTER EIGHT: SHORT-TERM GAINS VERSUS LONG-TERM SUCCESS

KEY TAKEAWAYS
- **False Sense of Urgency:**
  Short-term opportunities often create a sense of urgency that distracts from a bigger, more meaningful vision.
- **FOMO and Peer Pressure:**
  The temptation to "fit in" by following what others are doing can cloud judgment, leading to decisions that don't align with personal values.

- **Strategic Decision-Making:**
  Focus on long-term alignment when evaluating opportunities rather than jumping on the latest trends or deals. A clear vision helps you discern opportunities that serve your goals from those that distract you.
- **Long-Term Vision:**
  Creating a long-term vision enables you to navigate short-term decisions with clarity and purpose, aligning with your ultimate goals.
- **The Value of Saying No:**
  Choosing to say no to opportunities that don't serve your long-term vision helps you prioritize the most important goals.
- **Aligned Experimentation:**
  Short-term opportunities can be valuable learning experiences if approached with an experimental mindset aligned with long-term goals.
- **Building Real NIL Value:**
  NIL value is more than just financial gain; it's about cultivating influence, leadership, and partnerships that align with your personal brand. Long-term NIL success is built from a foundation of clarity, authenticity, and alignment with your values.

DISCUSSION QUESTIONS

1. Think about a time when you were tempted by "shiny objects" (a deal, trend, or opportunity) that seemed too good to pass up.
2. How did you navigate the decision? What role did your core values and long-term vision play in your choice? How

can you develop more discernment in the future to avoid distractions?
3. What does your long-term vision for your NIL look like? Have you defined where you're going and where you're growing?
4. What specific steps can you take today to move closer to your long-term goals, rather than focusing on short-term rewards?

ACTION ITEM

Create a Long-Term Vision Statement: Take time to draft a personal vision statement that includes your values, desired impact, and your long-term goals for your athlete's NIL and beyond. Reflect on how the current opportunities you are facing together fit within that vision. Use this statement as a filter for future decision-making, ensuring that your choices contribute to building your lasting legacy, not just immediate wins.

CHAPTER NINE: DON'T LEAVE POTENTIAL ON THE TABLE

KEY TAKEAWAYS

- **Intrinsic Value Over External Validation:**
  Self-worth should not rely on external scorecards like social media engagement, sports accolades, or corporate metrics. "Athletes often fall into the trap of chasing external metrics, losing sight of their intrinsic value in the process."
- **Parental Influence:**
  Parents are uniquely positioned to affirm their child's inherent value, offering perspective that transcends external judgments.

- **Resilience over Rescue:**
Facing and learning from setbacks is crucial for long-term growth and success. "True growth happens when parents allow their children to encounter and overcome difficulties, cultivating their inner strength."
- **Avoiding Common Pitfalls:**
Comparison culture, time management challenges, catastrophic thinking, and contract naivety are common hurdles for student athletes that parents can help navigate.
- **Building Identity Beyond Sports:**
NIL opportunities serve as a platform for athletes to expand their sense of self beyond sports, planting seeds of potential and building a "gain of identity."

DISCUSSION QUESTIONS

1. What external scorecards (e.g., social media likes, sports statistics) do you or your child rely on for validation? How do these metrics impact confidence, focus, or decision-making?
2. How do you currently affirm your child's value beyond their achievements?
3. How can NIL opportunities expand your athlete's identity beyond sports?
4. Reflect on a time when your encouragement helped your child overcome a challenge. What was the result?

ACTION ITEMS

1. **Intrinsic Value Brainstorm (Parent and Athlete Together):**
Take five minutes each to write down: Qualities you love about yourself beyond accomplishments. Qualities you

admire in each other that aren't tied to performance. Share and discuss how these traits shape your identities.
2. **NIL Identity Map**
   Create a simple identity web: At the center, write your athlete's name. Surround it with words describing passions, skills, and goals (outside of sports). Discuss how NIL opportunities could nurture these traits.

CHAPTER TEN: VALUES AND ALIGNMENT

KEY TAKEAWAYS
- **Core Values as the Foundation:**
  Your values are the pillars on which your personal platform stands. Clarifying your core values helps ensure that your actions and decisions align with who you truly are, setting the foundation for growth in both your personal and professional life.
- **Importance of Family Values:**
  For families, aligning on core values not only improves communication but also strengthens the family's bond. These shared values offer a stable foundation for growth and decision-making, both individually and collectively.
- **Values as Decision-Making Tools:**
  Core values serve as a guide in navigating complex decisions, especially those that impact relationships, school choices, and NIL opportunities. Staying true to your values during decision-making ensures that you live authentically and avoid compromising on what's most important.
- **Teaching Values Through Example:**
  Parents are encouraged to model their core values consistently rather than simply preaching them. Children learn

ULTIMATE WINNING SEASON-READER'S GUIDE

best through observation, and living out your values helps instill them more naturally.

DISCUSSION QUESTIONS

1. Reflecting on Personal Values: What are the top three nonnegotiable values that guide your life? How do these values influence your decisions in your personal and professional life?
2. Family Alignment: How do you and your spouse align your individual values to create a shared family foundation? What values do you share as a family? Ask your family, "Where are our values aligned, and where do we differ?" How might this alignment influence your approach to family decisions and NIL opportunities?
3. Modeling Values for Children: What are some specific ways you can model your core values for your children? How can you ensure that these values are instilled through your actions rather than just your words? Are you practicing your values consistently? Look back over the last month and identify areas where you might have compromised your values—and how this impacted your sense of fulfillment.
4. Your Athlete's NIL and Brand Building: How do your core values influence your approach to NIL opportunities? Are there any partnerships or endorsements that your athlete would avoid based on your values?

ACTION ITEM

Daily Values Check-In: For the next week, track how often your actions align with your top five values. You can do this on a personal level or with your family to discuss your shared family values. Each day, ask:

- Did my actions today reflect my core values?
- What areas did I act in alignment with my values?
- Where did I compromise or stray from my values?

CHAPTER ELEVEN: RELATIONSHIPS

KEY TAKEAWAYS

- **Relationships as Levers for Growth:**
Personal and professional growth cannot be achieved in isolation. Relationships push you to grow through challenges and feedback for emotional maturity, communication, and leadership development.
- **Growth Comes Through Collaboration, Not Competition:**
In today's VUCA world, building mutually beneficial relationships is key to long-term success. Relationships allow for opportunities where everyone wins.
- **Mentorship Plays a Crucial Role:**
A mentor serves as a steady, guiding influence that helps you stay aligned with your purpose and overcome challenges.
- **Investing in Relationships Creates Exponential Impact:**
The more intentional and purpose-driven your relationships, the greater the growth and success you will experience.
- **Student Athletes Have a Unique Opportunity to Leverage Relationships:**
They can build meaningful, long-term relationships with teammates, coaches, mentors, and parents that will positively influence both their athletic and professional futures.

ULTIMATE WINNING SEASON–READER'S GUIDE

DISCUSSION QUESTIONS

1. Establishing trust: In what ways can you create an environment of open communication and trust with your child during their college transition?

2. Reflect on your own current relationships: How do they support or challenge your personal growth? Are there relationships that need more investment or boundaries for you to grow? How are they helping or hindering being a relationship role model for your child?

3. Think about mentorship: Does your athlete have a mentor in their life who serves as a "third person"? How has their guidance impacted them? If not, how can you start seeking out aligned mentorship to help your athlete navigate their journey?

4. In what ways do you approach collaboration versus competition? How can you shift your mindset or approach to relationships to ensure collaborative success for your student athlete?

ACTION ITEM

Identify three key relationships in your athlete's life (personal, professional, or athletic). Reflect on how these relationships can support their growth. Then, set a plan to intentionally nurture one of these relationships in the next month, whether by investing more time, providing support, or setting clear boundaries for healthier interaction.

CHAPTER TWELVE: WHAT DOES SUCCESS LOOK LIKE?

KEY TAKEAWAYS
- **Defining Success in the Short Versus Long Term:**
Success can be seen as a series of incremental wins—like NIL deals or athletic accomplishments—but true success is achieved when these are complemented by personal growth, leadership, and the ability to adapt to life after sports.
- **Success for Parents:**
A parent's success is measured by watching their student athlete grow into their full potential, both in sports and in life. Parents are encouraged to adopt a long-term view, helping their child develop the resilience, skills, and mindset needed for future leadership.
- **Success for Student Athletes:**
Student athletes' definitions of success are often shaped by their immediate sports goals, such as NIL opportunities and athletic achievements, but they must also prepare for life after sports. Continuous growth is the key: avoiding complacency and embracing a mindset of limitless potential.
- **Vertical Growth over Time:**
Success should evolve beyond technical skills and achievements (horizontal growth) into deeper life skills, leadership, and personal development (vertical growth). Vertical growth helps individuals navigate life transitions and remain adaptable, ensuring long-term success after the sports career ends.
- **Preparing for Success Beyond Sports:**
While achieving athletic goals is important, true success involves preparing for life after sports by developing a platform that can be leveraged for entrepreneurial opportunities, leadership, relationships, and mentorship.

- **The Role of Faith:**
  Faith provides stability and purpose when navigating life transitions. Whether in moments of victory or adversity, it helps maintain perspective and focus on long-term growth while staying true to core values.

DISCUSSION QUESTIONS

1. How do you define success for your child in the long term? How do you support their growth while letting them pursue their own path? How do your current parenting strategies help or potentially hinder your student athlete's development?

2. In what ways might your own definition of success be limiting or potentially pressuring your student athlete's authentic growth and potential?

3. What personal fears or unresolved experiences from your own athletic or academic journey might be unconsciously influencing how you support your child's path?

4. In what ways can you and your athlete incorporate both horizontal (skills acquisition) and vertical (personal growth) development into your life to ensure continuous improvement?

5. How do you help your child stay grounded in their values and identity through both victories and setbacks?

ACTION ITEMS

Parents, reflect on your role in shaping the long-term success of your child. What actions can you take to ensure they stay grounded, adaptable, and ready for life's challenges beyond sports?

Balance Short-Term Wins with Long-Term Vision: Align athletic achievements, strengths, and short-term NIL activities with life goals and long-term vision by creating a through line that shows the connection, themes, and growth path your athlete would like to pursue as they become a leader inside and outside of sports.

CALL TO ACTION: NEXT STEP FOR YOUR JOURNEY

Now that you've reflected on your own role and actions as a parent, it's time to take the next step toward a **personalized plan** for your child's long-term success. Your investment today can build their platform for greatness tomorrow.

At **NIL Builders Group**, we specialize in guiding families just like yours through the journey of name, image, and likeness (NIL) success, leadership development, and entrepreneurial growth. Our team is equipped to help you create a strategic development plan for your student athlete and their personal brand. Here's what you can do next:

- **Book a Consultation:** Our **NIL Strategists** will help you assess your family's readiness for this unique journey and help you create an actionable plan.
- **Join Our Group Coaching:** Dive deeper into the development process by participating in our accelerator program.

This program will walk you through the essentials of building a successful, personalized NIL strategy, leadership principles, and personal branding. Join a cohort of like-minded parents and students to receive guidance, mentorship, and collaborative support.

- **Create a Personalized Action Plan:** Start right away by setting an appointment with one of our NIL experts. If you choose to work with us in developing your strategy, you'll receive a tailored roadmap that aligns your child's NIL potential with their passions, talents, and values. We'll take your family through the PLATFORMULA process to create a customized plan that covers NIL strategy, leadership growth, and actionable steps for fostering your child's long-term success.

Now is the time to invest in your child's greatness. Together, let's support their growth, their future, their influence, and their impact. Reach out to **NIL Builders Group** today to start creating your personalized journey toward success.

NEXT STEP ACTIONS

1. **Contact NIL Builders Group** for an initial consultation call.
2. **Join our Group Coaching Program** to accelerate your understanding of NIL strategies and leadership development.
3. **Set up a meeting with an NIL Strategist** to develop a personalized action plan for your student athlete.

By taking these next steps, you're setting your child up for success, both in the world of name, image, and likeness and in their personal growth. The opportunity to thrive in the ever-changing world of sports, entrepreneurship, and leadership is within reach. Let us help you jumpstart the legacy they deserve.

ABOUT THE AUTHOR

Neeley Neal blends unparalleled expertise in leadership development, sports marketing, and technology with the firsthand experience of an elite athlete who understands the grit and discipline required for long-term success.

With over twenty years of experience leading in tech platform innovation, sports marketing, brand partnerships, and high-performance team-building, Neeley channels her expertise into empowering student-athletes and their families to thrive in the rapidly changing landscape of college sports. As a mother of four—including triplets—she intimately understands the challenges of nurturing multiple paths to excellence while maintaining strong family values.

Some of the highlights of her decades-long career include the following:

- Award-winning founder, NIL Builders Group
- Keynote speaker and agile mindset consultant, specialized in leadership and team development across rapidly evolving tech and sports business industries

- Former marketing and technical product leader at GoDaddy, managing platform services, brand campaigns, global marketing and new customer acquisition strategy
- Worked with organizations such as the Atlanta Falcons, Arizona Cardinals, Chicago Bears, Ticketmaster, Fox Sports, Phoenix Suns, Texas Rangers, WNBA Sacramento Monarchs, Arizona State University Athletics, and Texas Christian University Athletics, among other collegiate and professional sports organizations
- Holds specialized graduate degrees (MBA) in sports business, strategic marketing and a bachelor's degree in economics
- Performed at Super Bowl XLIII and traveled to South Korea, Japan, Guam, Hawaii, Texas, and Washington in support of the United States military for Armed Forces Entertainment Tours, as an NFL cheerleader and captain for the Arizona Cardinals.
- Sought-after national and regional competition judge and events director for the United Spirit Association (USA) and Varsity Brands
- Certified Jon Gordon Speaker and Trainer for Power of Positive Leadership, Power of Positive Teams and Energy Bus workshops
- Featured in *Forbes*, *Disrupt Magazine*, and *Authority Magazine* among other publications

A former NFL cheerleader and competitive athlete, Neeley knows what it takes to excel at the highest levels of athletic performance and translate those lessons into meaningful opportunities beyond the game.

Through her work as a consultant, speaker, and community builder, Neeley has helped countless families navigate

ABOUT THE AUTHOR

the complex NIL landscape as a trusted advisor. Her proven frameworks for success bring sports families together to create life-changing leverage for your athlete to pursue professional opportunity, prosperity, and purpose. To connect with Neeley, visit her website at nilbuildersgroup.com.

www.ingramcontent.com/pod-product-compliance
Lightning Source LLC
Chambersburg PA
CBHW020241010526
44107CB00039B/1455/J